learn to MACHINE QUILT with Pat Sloan

Dear Reader,

When I started quilting I learned to make quilts entirely by hand — from hand piecing and appliqué to hand quilting. Because I have always enjoyed using my sewing machine, I very quickly replaced my hand piecing and appliqué with machine work. I soon realized that I loved to make quilts, lots and lots of quilts, which meant I needed to learn how to free-motion machine quilt my quilt tops.

At that time, the free-motion method of quilting swirls and curves was very new in my area. After trying it, free-motion quilting just seemed to feel right to me and quickly became my signature style. Quilt shop owners began asking me to teach free-motion quilting. This book is based on the class I designed and still teach. The approach is easy, fast-paced, full of information, and will have you quilting free-motion swirls, curves, and other shapes in no time!

As I open the door for you, I hope you will step through into my world of free-motion machine quilting, where you will soon be making wonderful, finished quilts. Come on, you can do it!

Happing Quilting!

Pat

LEISURE ARTS, INC.
Little Rock, AR

a little more
ABOUT ME

For years, I worked as a computer programmer. When I discovered quilting, the word "software" took on a whole new meaning for me. Over the years I have become well known for my whimsical, folksy appliqué patterns and my fabric lines. I have designed and produced dozens of wall hangings, placemats, table runners, lap quilts, and bed quilts.

When I am not in my studio designing, I am answering e-mails from quilters, teaching and traveling to trade shows, guild meetings and lectures. When asked what I do for a living I reply, "I design and make quilts, which is a pretty wonderful job!" To see more of my patterns, books, and fabrics, visit my Website at www.quiltershome.com.

& ABOUT *my*CLASS

(FROM LEFT) LINDA TIANO, JEAN LEWIS, FRANCES HUDDLESTON, PAT SLOAN, CHERYL JOHNSON, NELWYN GRAY, AND LISA LANCASTER

After the overwhelming success of my previous class and book, *Learn to Appliqué with Pat Sloan*, I was thrilled when I was asked to return to Leisure Arts to teach a machine quilting workshop. The Quilt Department staff and I eagerly anticipated the fun, friendship, and sharing of knowledge this class would provide. And we were not disappointed!

Now, YOU are invited to join our group as I introduce you to my favorite tools and supplies, explain how to prepare a top for quilting, and instruct you in my signature style of free-motion machine quilting. After working on some practice pieces and an easy project or two, you will soon find yourself—as the class members did—free-motion machine quilting with confidence!

my favorite
TOOLS & SUPPLIES

- BATTING

- BASTING SUPPLIES

- SEWING MACHINE NEEDLES

- THREAD

- "HELPER" TOOLS

- SEWING MACHINES AND WORKSPACES

In addition to the basic sewing supplies, there are numerous products available for machine quilting. The tools and supplies described below are ones that I have tried and found perform well or make the quilting process easier.

BATTING

Over the years I've found that most sewing machines will "needle" through any type of batting. Therefore, choose your batting based on your quilting design (how far apart you plan to quilt) and the look and feel you want the quilt to have after it has been quilted. Battings are available in many different thicknesses, called lofts. The higher the loft, the fluffier your quilt will feel and the less it will drape.

Tip: I suggest quilting a small test sample to see if you like an unfamiliar batting before using it in a quilt.

POLYESTER BATTING

Many quilters start out using polyester batting, but I think most of us switch to another type of batting after the first few quilts. "Poly" has a tendency to "beard," which means the fibers come out through the holes the quilting has made. It can be bulky to deal with under the presser foot and just doesn't have the soft drape of cotton battings. One poly that I *do* like students to try is Hobbs Thermore® Ultra Thin Batting. This batting is very thin, doesn't beard, and isn't bulky under the presser foot.

100% COTTON BATTING

The length of the cotton fibers used for making batting dictates how far apart you will need to quilt. Batting made from traditional, short cotton fibers will require quilting about every 2 inches to prevent shifting and tearing of the batting when a quilt is used. An example of this type of batting is Mountain Mist® Blue Ribbon. I do love the crinkly, antique look and authentic feel this type of batting gives to reproduction quilts after they are washed.

Battings made from longer cotton fibers do not need to be quilted as closely. You can leave as much as 6 to 12 inches between quilting lines. Right out of the bag these battings feel different from ones made from short fibers, some of them are as soft as baby blankets already! Examples include Mountain Mist® Cream Rose and White Rose and Quilters Dream Cotton. Some Hobbs and Fairfield cotton battings also allow more space between the quilting. Check package labels to see how far apart the manufacturer suggests you quilt.

FUSIBLE BATTING

Fusible battings come in both a poly/cotton blend and 100% cotton. I like Mountain Mist® Gold-Fuse which is a 50/50 blend. It is very thin and feels like 100% cotton after quilting. The fusible adhesive is very light and you can reposition the batting while basting if needed. My sewing machine needle never gums up when using this product.

Mountain Mist® makes a 100% cotton version called White-Gold. Several other companies also make fusible battings. Whichever brand you use, be sure to follow manufacturer's instructions and be sure to quilt a test piece before using it in your quilt.

WOOL BATTING

I really love wool batting. Wool batting is fluffy and light, not dense and heavy like the wool used in coats. The fluff adds dimension to quilting designs with open spaces. Wool seems to release fold lines better than cotton and many competition quilts are now being made with wool batting for that reason. An example of a wool batting is Hobbs Heirloom® Washable Wool. There are also many independent companies which produce wool batting — some even raise their own sheep!

OTHER BATTING OPTIONS

Some other options include wool/poly blends and even 100% silk. If a batting is very expensive, like silk, I suggest you try a small sample to see if you really like it better than the traditional options for the type of quilting you are doing.

BASTING SUPPLIES
The quilt top, batting, and backing (quilt sandwich) must be held together securely (basted) while you are machine quilting. I suggest pin-basting, spray-basting, fusible batting, or basting guns.

QUILTER'S BASTING PINS
I like to use 1" long safety pins, either curved or straight. I store my pins open in an old canning jar. I leave the pins open, because you need them to be open when pin-basting and when removing them from a quilt; they are ready to use again thus avoiding a repeated motion.

Tip: If you have children, always keep the jar lid on and store the jar on a top shelf.

Tip: After buying a new box of pins, test them before adding them to a current pin collection. Twice, I have purchased pins that would not slide through a quilt sandwich. Once you dump those "duds" in with your good pins, it will take years to find all the bad ones — just ask me how I know!

BASTING SPRAYS
There are many brands of spray adhesives available to choose from and they usually work well for small projects. Be sure to follow the manufacturer's instructions when using these products.

Tip: One of the downfalls of using an aerosol product is over-spray, but working outside or in a restricted, covered area will help.

FUSIBLE BATTING
I really like using fusible batting for large quilts because you don't have to quilt around pins and it is easy to handle. You will need a large flat surface to assemble and fuse a quilt sandwich. I like to use my bedroom floor. Steam is needed to activate the glue in the fusible batting, so laying it out on the carpeting works fine. Another advantage to using fusible batting is that you can reposition it, if needed, when assembling the quilt sandwich.

BASTING GUNS
Basting guns shoot plastic tacks, similar to the ones used to attach clothing labels, through the layers of the quilt sandwich. The tacks are not reusable, but they are easy to remove.

SEWING MACHINE NEEDLES

I use good quality #70 or #80 standard (universal) needles.

Tip: I buy bulk boxes of 100 needles. They are less expensive in bulk, and because you have them, you are more likely to change the needle when you should. Most sewing centers can order them for you. You could share a box with a friend.

Specialty needles, such as quilting needles with very sharp, tapered points, metallic needles for use with metallic thread, and embroidery needles with larger eyes for use with rayon thread are usually more expensive than standard machine needles, but you may want to try them. Some quilters feel specialty needles work better with their sewing machines.

THREAD

It is very important to use a high quality thread. Bargain brand thread tends to break easily while quilting and often creates a lot of lint in the bobbin case.

THREAD WEIGHTS AND FIBER CONTENT

I usually use 100% cotton or rayon thread when quilting. Thread is available in various weights (40, 50, or 60). When selecting thread remember, the higher the number… the finer the thread. 50-weight is usually considered the standard weight when machine quilting.

Tip: Quilters are often taught to use 100% cotton thread when sewing on 100% cotton fabric. The reason for this is, if a quilt is used, tugged, pulled, and loved, there is a lot of tension on the thread and fabric. If you have used cotton thread, it will break under the strain and you'll just need to repair the quilting. If you have used a synthetic thread (polyester, rayon, metallic, etc.) or silk, the thread won't break, but the fabric will tear. It is much more difficult to fix torn fabric than broken thread. If your quilt will not be washed or handled often, any type thread can be used for quilting.

SPECIALTY THREADS

These threads add sparkle and fun to your quilt! Variegated thread can be made from 100% cotton, a blend, or synthetic fibers. Other specialty threads include metallics and monofilament.

BOBBIN THREAD

Most of the time when using cotton thread you will use the same thread in the top and bobbin. When using synthetic specialty threads, I like to use a standard 50-weight cotton thread in the bobbin. For example, if I am using a 40-weight green variegated rayon thread for quilting, I use a medium green 50-weight cotton thread in the bobbin.

THREAD COLOR

Matching - I often match the color of the thread to the fabric so it blends to give texture and does not stand out as a feature (**Fig. 1**). An example is using blue thread on blue backgrounds, red on red flowers, and green on green leaves.

Tip: When you are a beginner, use thread that matches the fabrics in the quilt top for your quilting *and* in the bobbin. Also, using a floral cotton fabric for your backing will allow the different thread colors to blend in so that any uneven stitching will not stand out.

Blending - The downside to using matching thread is that you have to change thread frequently. Many times you can find a neutral color that blends well with most of the fabrics in your quilt top (**Fig. 2**). When using neutral thread you won't have to change colors as often or maybe even not at all. For example, use a medium brown or dark tan thread on a red and tan quilt.

Contrasting - Most specialty threads will be a high contrast to the quilt top. I love to use the variegated threads for backgrounds and details so that the colors fade in and out (**Fig. 3**). Do a test to be sure *you* like how it looks before starting on your quilt.

Tip: I outline quilt around appliqués with a thread color that matches the background fabric. I usually find the color changes in variegated thread too distracting for outline quilting.

fig. 1

fig. 2

fig. 3

"HELPER" TOOLS

When I first started free-motion quilting there were no "helper" tools, but now there are several. The tools or supplies listed below are ones that either I use or my students have found very useful.

SAFETY PIN GRIP COVERS

These plastic covers snap over one side of your safety pins and give you a larger area to hold when pin-basting. They are available in a wide variety of sizes.

SPRING CLAMPS

I use spring clamps to anchor the backing to a table when pin-basting (**Fig. 4**). They are available at hardware stores and I prefer them to binder clips (hard to open wide) or picnic table clamps (usually not a tight grip).

fig. 4

KWIK-KLIP™

This is my "must-have" tool for closing safety pins when pin-basting (**Figs. 5** and **6**). After inserting a basting pin through the layers of your quilt sandwich, use the slot in the tip of the Kwik-Klip to push the pin up and close it. This tool will save time, sore fingers, and broken fingernails.

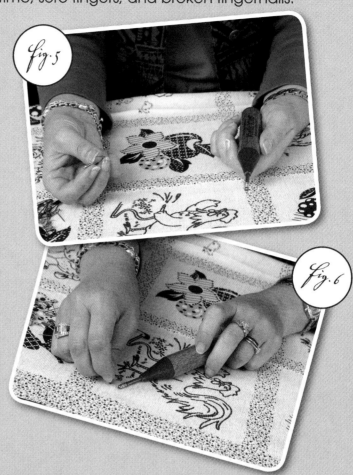

fig. 5

fig. 6

MAGNIFIER

Magnifiers can either be freestanding or attach to your sewing machine and most have a light. When quilting a small area, a magnifier will really help you to see your stitches.

QUILTING GLOVES

Some quilters find that the fabric feels slippery and they don't have complete control when stitching. Wearing specially made quilting gloves or garden gloves with rubber fingertips may help. However, gloves can be bulky and you might have to keep removing them to handle tasks such as clipping threads or removing pins.

Tip: Some quilters find using a slightly tacky hand lotion will keep their hands from slipping when stitching.

SEWING MACHINES AND WORKSPACES

Any sewing machine used for free-motion quilting must be able to produce a nice, uniform stitch, even when using different top and bobbin threads. It must be in good working order and able to run for extended periods of time without overheating. With the exception of the first two items, the following features are not absolutely necessary, but having them may make your machine quilting easier and more enjoyable.

SEWING MACHINE FEATURES

*   **Feed dog control -** Most machines allow you to drop (lower) the feed dogs (**Fig. 7**), while some machines have a special throat plate to cover the feed dogs. While you *can* free-motion quilt with feed dogs raised, I do not recommended it...just ask me how I know!

fig. 7

*   **Special quilting feet -** You will need a walking foot for straight-line quilting and a darning or quilting foot for free-motion quilting. I find that feet designed for your particular machine are usually the best (check with your manufacturer), but you might find generic ones that will work.

There are several types of darning feet available (**Fig. 8**). Among them are, small metal closed or open-toe circles, large metal circles, clear plastic circles, and squares. I prefer using a small metal closed foot because, when quilting, I am not looking into the center of the foot...I am always looking ahead to where I "will be."

fig. 8

*   **Needle down option -** With this function the needle always stops in the fabric so you never lose your stitching place. It is also handy when you need to pivot or make adjustments to the quilt sandwich. If your machine does not have this option, you may be able to "kick or tap" the needle down with the foot pedal.

Tip: If you can't kick or tap the needle down, you may be able to upgrade to a foot petal that will allow you to perform this step. It is very important to stop with the needle down as the quilt may shift.

- **Machine bed extension -** You will need a large surface to rest your left hand on and to support the weight of the quilt (**Fig. 9**). Usually the machine bed extension table that comes with a sewing machine is a bit small. I have an after market table which replaces the original one. If your machine is in a cabinet or sits flush with your sewing machine table, you will more than likely have enough table space.

fig. 9

- **Hands-free presser foot lifter -** Some machines have a function that will automatically raise the presser foot when you are in the needle down position and stop stitching. Others machines have a presser foot knee lift—either option will give you more control over your quilting because you don't have to remove your hands from the quilt.
- **Autopilot -** This feature lets you run the machine without pressing the foot petal, providing a steady speed that allows you more control over your stitch length. If you don't have this option, with practice, you can develop a consistent foot control speed.
- **Empty bobbin warning -** A beeper will sound when your bobbin is almost empty, allowing you time to maneuver to a good stopping point on your quilt to replace the bobbin.

WORKSPACE ERGONOMICS

- It is very important to have a good, supportive chair to use when quilting. Most office chairs work well because you can tilt the seat and raise or lower it to the right height. I find I prefer a chair without arms.
- To test your chair and sewing table position, sit in front of your sewing machine with feet flat on the floor. Your back, upper legs and lower legs should all be at exact 90° right angles. Place your hands on the sewing machine bed, with palms flat on either side of the needle. Your elbows should be bent at an exact 90° right angle (**Fig. 10**). If they are not, you might experience shoulder pain when quilting for extended periods. Raise or lower your chair or sewing table as needed to achieve the right ergonomics.
- No matter how comfortable your workspace is, it is a good idea to get up, stretch, and move around for a few minutes every hour to help reduce muscle fatigue.

Tip: For a change of position, you might try placing your machine on a high counter and standing to quilt. Remember to keep your back straight and your arms at the same 90° right angles as when sitting.

fig. 10

QUILTING

*Because the quilting process involves many interrelated steps, please read the entire **Quilting** section, pages 11-31, before beginning a project.*

PLANNING YOUR QUILTING

To me, the design of a quilt has two parts...the "pattern" you make with fabric placement and the "pattern" you make with quilting stitches. Quilting stitches can enhance the look of a quilt in a major way or they can just hold the layers together. There are thousands of "patterns" you can create when machine quilting, so start by asking yourself some questions.

- How much time do I want to spend quilting this project?
- Will it be an heirloom?
- Will it be functional or decorative?
- Is it for a gift or for myself?

Once you know the level of effort you want to expend, it's time to think about how to quilt your top....

- If you don't want to spend a lot of time quilting, there is the "I'm glad it is almost done" approach. Choose a large overall design or even just straight lines. The quilting will still enhance the piece, but requires minimal stitching.
- For the "I want to do a medium amount of quilting" approach, look at the design of the quilt top. For a pieced quilt, you could outline the pattern of the blocks or use an overall design across the quilt. For appliquéd quilts, try outlining the appliqués and heavily quilting the backgrounds.
- Then, there is the "I want the very best" approach. You may wish to quilt heavily, change thread colors often, use marked designs, and even include fancy motifs like feathers and wreaths. Your machine quilting could take as long as it took to make the top!

11

TYPES OF QUILTING

While I love free-motion quilting in my very unstructured style, I have included descriptions of some other types of quilting I also use when quilting.

FREE-MOTION

The most fun style of quilting in the world! Free-motion designs can be semi-planned or totally unplanned. You can cover the entire surface of a quilt (washing), fill in backgrounds behind appliqués, or use in borders. Some of my favorite free-motion designs include:

- Loops and swirls (**Fig. 11**)

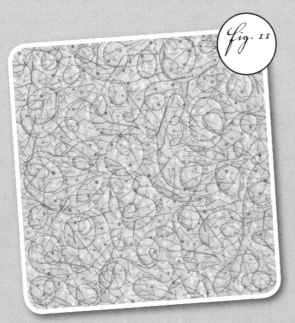

- Connected triangles (**Fig. 12**)

- Swirls that connect other shapes, such as hearts, flowers, stars, and even names (**Fig. 13**)

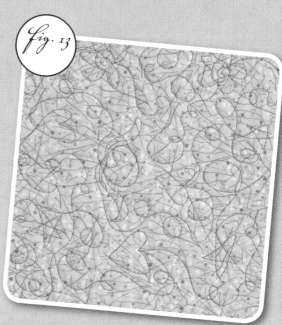

- Vines with leaves and flowers (**Fig. 14**)

- Large shapes (like a cabbage rose or a big leaf) that connect, change size, and repeat across the surface (**Fig. 15**)

- Bubbles (**Fig. 17**)

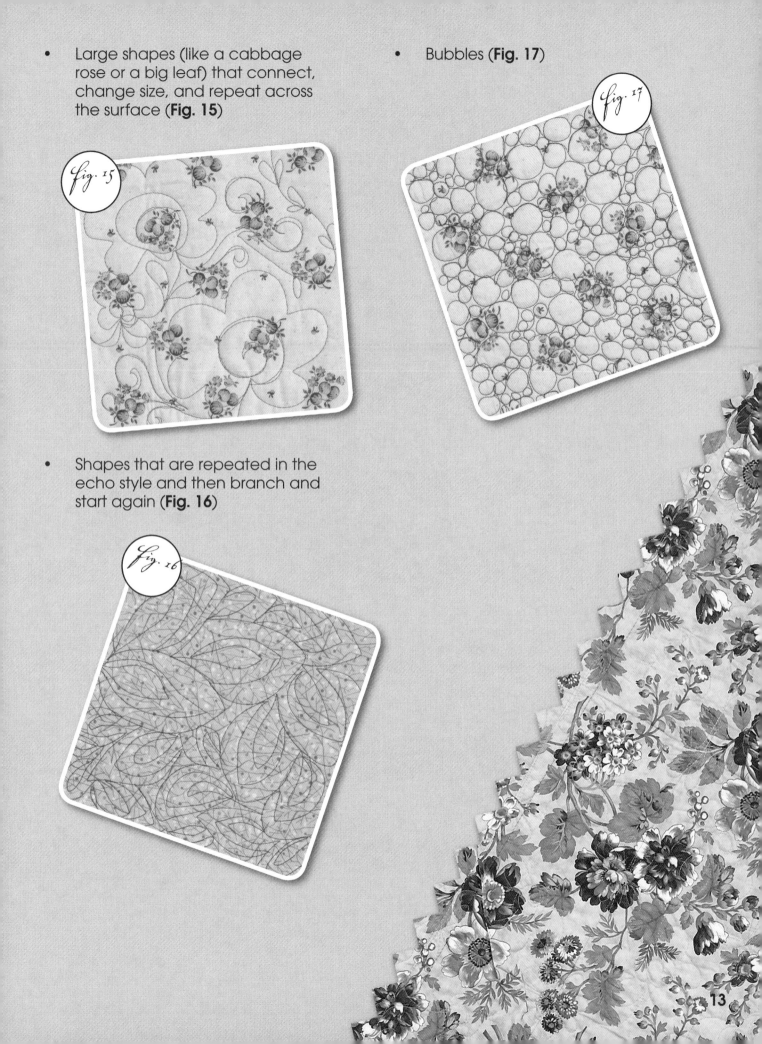

- Shapes that are repeated in the echo style and then branch and start again (**Fig. 16**)

STIPPLING

Stippling is a style of free-motion quilting which forms a dense, random design that does not cross itself (**Fig. 18**). It is often used for filling in backgrounds. The "not crossing itself" is the part that makes this technique less fun for most people.

Note: I have taught free-motion quilting to hundreds of quilters over the years and one of the most often asked questions is about stippling. It seems that stippling has become known as the "only" machine quilting allowed. Thank goodness it's not true! Stippling is just a style of quilting!

IN-THE-DITCH

This type of quilting is usually stitched using a walking foot. You stitch in the seam allowance between pieced blocks, between sections of a block, or between the quilt top center and borders (**Fig. 19**). Generally this type of quilting holds the layers together, but does not add anything to the design. I use in-the-ditch to stabilize the quilt sandwich before I begin free-motion quilting.

OUTLINE

I look at outline quilting as "what is done to make appliqué shapes pop off the surface of a quilt." I outline quilt as close to the edges of appliqués as possible with thread that matches the background color. You can also use outline quilting in pieced designs where you want to accent a shape (**Fig. 20**). Leaving the center of the shape un-quilted will make it pop.

SHAPE ENHANCERS

I quilt inside appliqué shapes (**Fig. 21**) or any large open areas of pieced blocks to enhance or add details to the shape. Examples include quilting veins in leaves, adding petals to large flowers, quilting inside the roof of a house, or putting a swirl inside the center of a pieced star.

Tip: Quilting designs need to be balanced and have an even density across the whole quilt. If you have quilted heavily in the background, then you need to quilt inside larger shapes so they don't "puff" and look incomplete.

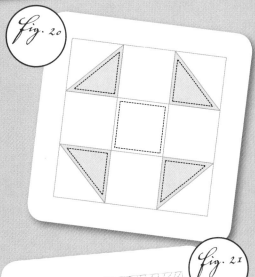

fig. 18

fig. 19

fig. 20

fig. 21

ECHO

Echo quilting is repeating evenly spaced lines of quilting around an appliqué or pieced shape several times (**Fig. 22**). It can also be the repeat of a shape you have quilted, such as a leaf.

fig. 22

MY MIX

I usually use a mix of background quilting and shape enhancers. For appliquéd quilts, I may do some outline quilting, lots of background quilting, and some special shapes such as flowers, circles, or stars in open areas. On a pieced quilt, I might outline pieced stars to make the points pop and then wash an all over free-motion design across the background.

MARKED DESIGNS

Any quilting stencil or pattern can be adapted for free-motion quilting, but I feel that following a marked design takes more time, practice, and just isn't as much fun. Also, the quilt top must be marked **before** layering your quilt and the markings will need to be removed when you are finished.

 Tip: If you choose to mark a design, always test your marking tool, to be sure the marks are easily removed, before using it on your quilt.

COLOR, PATTERN, AND QUILTING DESIGNS

I'd like to share a few tips on how color and fabric patterns influence my choice of quilting designs.

Heavily Patterned Fabric

When using dense floral or busy geometric fabrics, the quilting will hardly show. I usually do simple, basic quilting on patterned fabrics.

Dark-colored Fabrics

Whether dark fabric is patterned or not, it is hard to see the quilting when using a matching thread color. Once again, I do basic quilting, unless I want the quilting to really show and choose to use a high contrast thread.

Light-colored Fabrics

Machine quilting is most visible on light fabrics, with or without pattern. Here is the place I like to stitch those fancy flowers, free-form feathers, and add names and dates.

Tip: Using a high contrast thread color will allow most quilting to show up on light or dark fabrics, but it also *really* shows off your stitches — just something to think about.

THE ART OF "NOT" PLANNING A DESIGN

I prefer to do very little planning of my quilt designs. I have a basic style and I let that style do its thing on my quilts. Here are a few ways I quilt without planning:

- For appliqué quilts, I always outline the appliqué shapes. Then I stitch an all-over design in the background. Sometimes the quilt's theme gives me an idea, such as stitching leaves on a quilt with flower appliqués.
- I will often quilt a shape I see in the fabric. For example, if the quilt is made using a fish fabric, I might stitch water and fish.
- For pieced quilts, I like to wash large shapes across the surface, such as cabbage roses with leaves.
- Borders are fun because of their long skinny shape. I like stitching free-form feathers, repeating shapes, or echo quilting around a shape.
- If you MUST do a specific design, instead of marking the quilt top, try this method. Draw the design on tissue paper, pin or baste the paper to the quilt top and quilt through the paper. You will need to tear the paper off when you are finished quilting, but you won't have to test fabrics or remove marks.

DEVELOPING YOUR STYLE

As you are learning to free-motion quilt, you will find that certain shapes and patterns are visually appealing to you, are fun to stitch, and your quilting looks better! This becomes your signature style of quilting. Enjoy it, use it, and once you have mastered your signature style branch out to master a new style.

PREPARING A PROJECT FOR QUILTING

While you may want to jump right in and start quilting a queen-size quilt, I suggest you start with some practice squares and pre-printed quilt panels. Once you are comfortable quilting, try a small project such as a table runner or wall hanging.

MAKING A QUILT SANDWICH

The first steps in quilting include preparing, layering, and securing your quilt top, batting, and backing to make a quilt sandwich.

Backing and Batting

1. Measure the length and width of your quilt top and cut your backing at least 6" longer and 6" wider than your quilt top. Follow **Steps 2-3**, if needed, to piece a backing for a large quilt.

Tip: If you skimp when cutting your backing, you might find that by the time you are basting the last corner of a big quilt, you don't have any backing on that corner because the layers were not perfectly aligned or shifted slightly. When this happens to me, I just sew a triangle of fabric to the corner of the backing and finish basting...really!

2. If your quilt top width is over 34" but less than 79", cut your backing fabric into two lengths slightly longer than the determined **length** measurement. Trim the selvages and sew the long edges together, forming a tube (**Fig. 23**). Match the seams and press along one fold (**Fig. 24**). Cut along the pressed fold to form a single piece (**Fig. 25**).

3. If your quilt top width is more than 79", it may require less fabric if the backing is pieced horizontally. Divide the **length** measurement by 40" to determine how many widths are needed. Cut the required number of widths the determined **width** measurement. Trim the selvages and sew the long edges together to form a single piece.

4. Trim the backing to the size determined in **Step 1**; press the seam allowances open. Press the entire backing.

5. To remove fold lines from packaged batting, spread it over a large flat surface overnight or use your air-dry setting on your dryer to fluff batting.

6. Cut your batting the same size as your backing, unless you plan to quilt in sections as I did my **Butterfly Garden Quilt**, page 60.

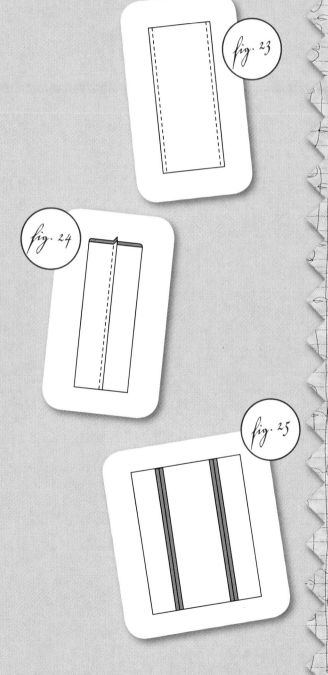

fig. 23

fig. 24

fig. 25

Layering

1. When layering, you will need to work on the largest flat surface you can find. A rectangular dining or folding table usually works well. If possible, the work surface should be just slightly smaller than your backing. If you don't have a table big enough, **Steps 3-7**, page 19, explain how to shift a quilt when pin-basting.

Tip: You might ask your local quilt shop, community center, or church if they have any large tables you can use.

Tip: Because you will be pinning through all the quilt layers, be sure to protect your tabletop from damage.

fig. 26

2. Matching wrong sides, fold your backing in half lengthwise. Place the folded edge in the center of your work surface. Unfold and allow the excess to hang off each side of your work surface (**Fig. 26**).

3. Spacing clamps about 12" apart, clamp one edge of your backing to the work surface (**Fig. 27**).

fig. 27

Note: When working on a large quilt, you may find it easier to place your first clamp in the center of one long edge of your work surface. Work from the center out to place remaining clamps.

4. On the opposite side, pull the backing tight without distorting the grainline; clamp along the work surface edge. Continue pulling and clamping along the length of your work surface. I find that I only need to clamp the two long sides, but you can clamp all four.

fig. 28

Tip: If your backing is much smaller than your tabletop, you can use masking tape, in place of clamps, to secure the edges.

5. Fold the batting in half lengthwise and place folded edge on the center of the backing; unfold and smooth out.

6. Matching right sides, fold the quilt top in half lengthwise and place the folded edge on the center of the batting; unfold and smooth out. The batting, backing, and quilt top should now be centered, layered, and ready to pin-baste (**Fig. 28**).

Pin-Basting

1. Start in the center and work outward in quadrants, placing pins about every 4". Try not to place pins where you know you will be quilting, for example, across seamlines. If an area of your quilt top does not lie completely flat, do not stretch or pull quilt top, just ease in the fullness as you pin (**Fig. 29**).

2. If your entire quilt top fits on your work surface, continue pin-basting until it is completely pinned and skip to **Step 8**.

3. If your quilt top is too large to fit on your work surface it will need to be shifted after you have pin-basted the available surface area.

4. Remove the clamps and pull the quilt sandwich (all three layers) in one direction until as much new area as possible is on the work surface.

5. Re-clamp the sandwich along the pinned side (**Fig. 30**).

fig. 29

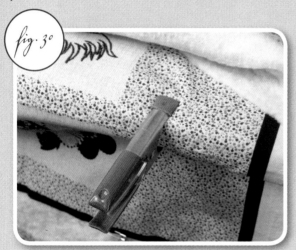

fig. 30

6. On the opposite side, pull the backing tight at the center; clamp. Spacing clamps about 12" apart, work from the center out to place clamps along the length of the backing. Pull the batting and quilt top smooth. Pin-baste the new area.

7. Continue moving the quilt sandwich and pin-basting until the entire quilt has been pin-basted.

8. When I am finished pin-basting the quilt sandwich, I pin-baste around the very edge of the quilt sandwich. This is very important for a large quilt, see my **Tip** (right).

Tip: I once rolled my sewing machine chair over the edge of a quilt and didn't know it. When I tried to move the quilt, I pulled the batting out of the sandwich in one spot! This problem could have been avoided if the edges had been pinned.

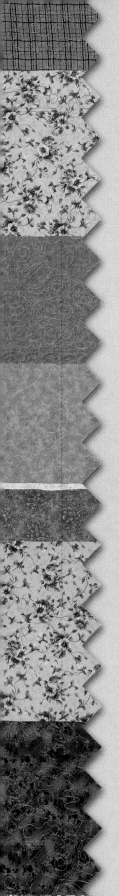

STITCHING A GRID

For quilts larger than about 40" x 40", I stitch a grid in-the-ditch to anchor the top, batting, and backing and prevent shifting as I free-motion quilt.

1. To grid your quilt, use your walking foot and thread that matches the background of your quilt top.
2. Set your stitch length for approximately 11 stitches to the inch.
3. Each section of the grid should outline an area about 12" to 18" square or rectangular. For quilts with pieced blocks, this is easy — just stitch in-the-ditch between the blocks. For quilts with appliqué, you might have to sew partial grids, stopping at or going around the appliqués **(Fig. 31)**.
4. Stitch in-the-ditch between the borders and the quilt top center. If you have pieced borders, you can grid those, too.
5. Remove the pins that are inside the grid. For borders that are not pieced or in areas where your top was not flat, leave the pins in until you are quilting in those sections.

fig. 31

Tip: Leaving pins in the areas that are not flat and in the borders will help you ease the fullness when machine quilting.

PREPARING THE EDGES

The backing and batting that extend beyond the quilt top can accidentally be folded under when machine quilting and sewn right to the back of your quilt — I've done this more than once! Now I prepare the edges to prevent this from happening.

1. Attach a zigzag foot to your machine.
2. Removing the edge pins as you go, sew a narrow, widely spaced zigzag around the outside edge of the quilt sandwich.
3. Trim the extra batting and backing 1" wider than the quilt top.

PREPARING YOUR MACHINE

1. Thread your machine.
2. Fill several bobbins to keep from having to stop and re-fill while quilting.
3. Drop or cover the feed dogs.
4. Select needle down option, if available.

5. Attach the darning foot and lower your presser foot. When lowered, there MUST be a space between the presser foot and throat plate. If you don't have a space, you may not have the right foot or your machine may have a "half way" position for the presser foot.

6. There is no stitch length setting for free-motion quilting. YOU become the regulator by the combination of your hand and foot speed. Some people like to set the length to zero, but I don't find any advantage to doing this.

BEGINNING TO STITCH

1. Place the quilt sandwich under the presser foot. If it does not fit easily into the arm opening of your machine, refer to **Bed Quilts**, page 30, to make a "quilt package."

2. Whenever possible, you will want to begin stitching near the center of your quilt top. If you have a pieced quilt top, starting in a ditch between seams will help hide your first stitches.

3. Once you have found a good starting point, lower your presser foot.

4. Pull the bobbin thread to the quilt surface by lowering the needle into the quilt sandwich, and then raising it. Lift the presser foot and tug on the top thread, pulling up the bobbin thread (**Fig. 32**).

fig. 32

Tip: When I try to eliminate Step 4, I sometimes end up with a big lump of thread on the back — not at all nice!

5. Lower the presser foot.

6. Holding the thread ends firmly, to keep them from being sucked into the bobbin case, take 4 or 5 stitches in place. This is your locking stitch.

7. Let go of the thread ends and begin stitching, keeping your hands on either side of the needle. After a few stitches, clip the thread ends even with the quilt surface.

Tip: If you are finding skipped stitches as you quilt, check to be sure you have lowered the presser foot.

8. Check the backing after a few stitches. The stitching on the back should look like the front. If there are loose loops of thread showing, (**Fig. 33**) adjust your tension. Try going to a higher number first. If this doesn't help, try a lower number. Continue testing to find the right tension for your machine and thread.

fig. 33

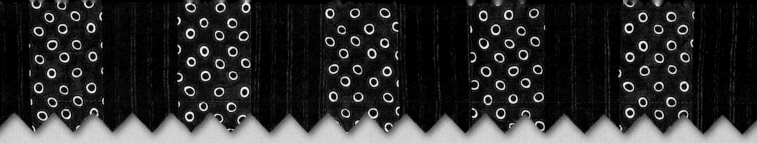

FREE-MOTION QUILTING

The whole free-motion quilting thing is just a few steps...but all done at the same time! Once your mind, hands, and feet are all working as one, free-motion quilting will become second nature. But until that happens you'll need to think about all these things to keep them going at the same time.

HAND CONTROL

*   As you move the quilt under the needle, the speed at which you move your hands regulates the stitch length.
*   Keep your hands on either side of the needle when you move the quilt (**Fig. 34**). You will need to stop and reposition your hands from time to time. This will become automatic with practice.
*   Remember to keep you arms at a 90° angle to your body (**Fig. 35**). When your arms are out-stretched, it's time to change your hand position!
*   Your goal is to make smooth consistent motions with your hands.

FOOT CONTROL

*   If you have a machine that runs on autopilot, now is the time to use this option! If the machine speed can be automatic then it is one less item for you to have to regulate.
*   Most machines do not have autopilot, so in addition to keeping your hand speed consistent, you must keep the speed of the machine consistent using the foot petal.
*   A faster foot speed is more forgiving of inconsistent hand speed. Once you are comfortable with controlling your hand speed, you might want to back down the speed of the machine.
*   If your machine has a half speed option, try using that to see if you like it.

fig. 34

fig. 35

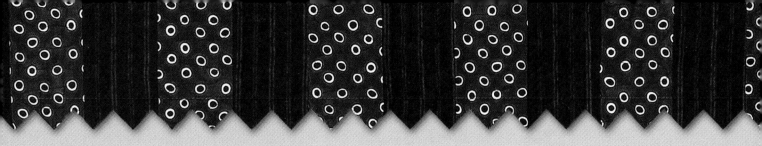

- I find that for open areas, quilting large shapes, or washing a design across the surface, I prefer to run the machine at a higher speed. This allows me to move my hands more quickly and finish quilting faster...gotta love that!
- When I'm outline quilting or quilting in small intricate areas, I slow down the speed of the machine *and* my hands. This gives me more control when moving the quilt.

FLOWING MOTION

- While running the machine, moving your hands at a consistent speed, and thinking about your design...your eyes need to be looking ahead to where you want to go...not where you have been or where you are now. Your eye is going to tell your hands where to move next.
- With free-motion quilting you can move from side to side, on the diagonal, or any direction. You don't need to turn the quilt as you do with straight-line quilting.
- The motion you want to create is smooth and gliding. If you are jerking from side to side, your curves will have points. Think smooth...practice this motion by placing a large scrap of cotton on a tabletop. Place both hands on the fabric and move it in a circular motion, creating swirls.
- When possible, move from one area to another by quilting along a seam, fabric edge, or over stitching you have already done. It is faster to keep quilting than to start and stop.

Tip: When outline quilting, you can sometimes save time by scooting into the appliqué, quilt your shape enhancers, and then return to outlining (**Fig. 36**).

fig 36

- Always try to maneuver to a seam to end your stitching or change bobbins.

Tip: If you have an empty bobbin sensor, you should have time to get to a seam for ending. Keep your bobbin area clean so that the sensor works properly.

fig. 37

fig. 38

DEALING WITH PINS

Hitting a safety pin can really damage your machine and it's not fun to sew a pin to the quilt top, which requires some tedious "unsewing." Here are my pin avoidance tips.

- Stitching a grid in your quilt sandwich allows you to remove most of the pins before you begin free-motion quilting.
- Quilt TOWARDS you so that you are quilting the area in front of the needle. Then you can see all the pins (**Fig. 37**).
- If you have to quilt away from you, behind the needle, stop and remove the pins first (**Fig. 38**). You cannot see the pins behind the needle.
- If you use fusible batting — NO pins! I love this option!

DRAG IS THE ENEMY

While quilting you want to keep most of the weight of the quilt up on your work area so that it doesn't pull against your machine.

fig. 39

- As you are stitching you will be shifting to new areas to quilt and will feel drag or pull on the quilt sandwich. You will need to stop and "fluff" the quilt by lifting and piling it on your sewing table or lap until it no longer drags (**Fig. 39**).
- For small-to medium-size quilts you won't have drag that often. If you have a large work area the quilt will just stay on the surface as you stitch.
- When you are working with a very large quilt, fluffing will be a constant process. You can put a chair to the left of your sewing table to help hold the quilt. Placing the back of your sewing table against a wall will keep the quilt from falling off the back.

TROUBLE SHOOTING

SKIPPED STITCHES

- Remove any lint from the bobbin case. When machine quilting, the thread and batting create a lot of lint. You will need to clean the bobbin area each time you insert a new bobbin.
- Be sure the presser foot is down.
- Change the needle. Your needle receives lots of wear and tear while machine quilting. Along with skipped stitches, a dull needle sometimes makes a popping sound as it enters the fabric.

Tip: Store broken or old needles in a small pill bottle. It's safe to throw away the closed pill bottle.

- Try a new spool of thread.

CURVES NOT SMOOTH

- Practice stitching large loops. As your curves become smoother, gradually decrease the size of your loops.
- Look at the back of the quilt. If the top thread is showing on the curves, try going slower. If it is still happening, adjust your tension to a higher number. If that doesn't help, adjust your tension to a lower number.
- If you cannot get the stitches to look the same on both sides (**Fig. 40**), you may need to have your machine serviced. It helps to show samples of the problem to a sewing machine mechanic.

THREAD IS SHREDDING

- Check to be sure your tension is correct.
- Try using a needle with a larger eye.

fig. 40

Tip: Any time you have to take your machine in to be serviced, test the repaired machine at the shop before taking it home.

THE VIRTURES OF PRACTICE

Just as it took you a little while to practice how to sew an accurate ¼" seam allowance or how to appliqué a smooth curve, it will take some practice to create consistent, even free-motion stitches.

PRACTICE SQUARES

1. Cut 8 squares 18" x 18" from muslin or another light-colored fabric. Cut 4 squares of batting 18" x 18".
2. Using your choice of basting methods, make 4 quilt sandwiches (**Fig. 41**).

fig. 4¹

Tip: Using fusible batting or basting spray to baste your practice squares and panels eliminates having to deal with pins as you are learning.

3. In order to see your stitches clearly, choose a high contrast thread.

Quilting Your Practice Squares

On these squares you will practice the feel of free-motion quilting and make tension adjustments. The arrows in the Figs. are to help you get a feel for the direction to move when quilting. Remember, you are not trying to recreate the pattern exactly — relax and have fun!

Square 1 - Loops

1. Following the arrows in **Fig. 42**, stitch loops. Try to maintain consistent hand and foot speed.
2. Stop and check the back of the square. Remember the stitches on the back should look very much like the ones on the front. If your stitches are too loose, adjust the tension slightly and try again.
3. Continue stitching loops and making adjustments until the stitch tension is the same on the front and back.

fig. 4²

Square 2 - Loops and Stars

1. Following the arrows in **Fig. 43**, stitch some loops and stars.

fig. 43

2. Check your stitch length. Are the stitches the same length? Work on maintaining consistent hand and foot speed.
3. Try adding some other simple shapes such as hearts or flowers (**Fig. 44**).

fig. 44

Tip: Remember when you are stitching to move the square side to side, diagonally, or forward and backward, as needed.

Square 3 - Flowers and Vines

1. Following the arrows in **Fig. 45**, stitch some large free-formed flowers, vines, and leaves.

fig. 45

Tip: If you would like, lightly draw some flowers and vines on your fabric. Practice following the drawn lines, but remember that they are only guides. You need to learn how it feels to just flow across the fabric.

2. Check your stitch length (**Fig. 46**).
   - If your stitches are too small, either move your hands faster or your foot speed slower.
   - If your stitches are too big, either move your hands slower or your foot speed faster.

fig. 46

3. Now try stitching some small free-formed flowers, vines, and leaves.

Square 4 - Outlining Shapes

1. Either draw or fuse a flower shape on your square.
2. Practice outlining the flower as if it were an appliqué (**Fig. 47**).
3. Fill in the background with bubbles (**Fig. 48**), swirls (**Fig. 49**), loops (**Fig. 50**), or any other design of your choosing.

fig. 47

Start/Stop

fig. 48

fig. 49

fig. 50

28

PRE-PRINTED PANELS

I love pre-printed quilt panels! When you practice on a panel, it allows you to practice on a quilt that you did not have to piece, gives you printed designs to follow, and can easily be finished into a usable project.

1. Cut a piece of batting and backing fabric at least 2" longer and 2" wider than your panel.
2. Using your choice of basting methods, make a quilt sandwich.

Quilting Your Panels

1. For panels with small prints or images, I like to do an all-over quilting design **(Fig. 51)**.
2. When a panel has large shapes, I like to outline the printed design.

Tip: After you finish quilting your panel, bind it and give it away! Yes, that's right, Get Rid Of It! You'll soon be thinking, "that was pretty good...I want to do another one!"

THE PROJECTS
Table Runners And Small Wall Hangings

- I suggest starting to quilt "real projects" with a table runner like **Sew Simple**, **(Fig. 52)** or small wall hanging like **Joy of Sewing**, **(Fig. 53)**. You won't have the issue of bulk and it won't take long to finish. Quilt several projects this size and when you are comfortable, move up to a lap size quilt.

fig. 51

fig. 52

fig. 53

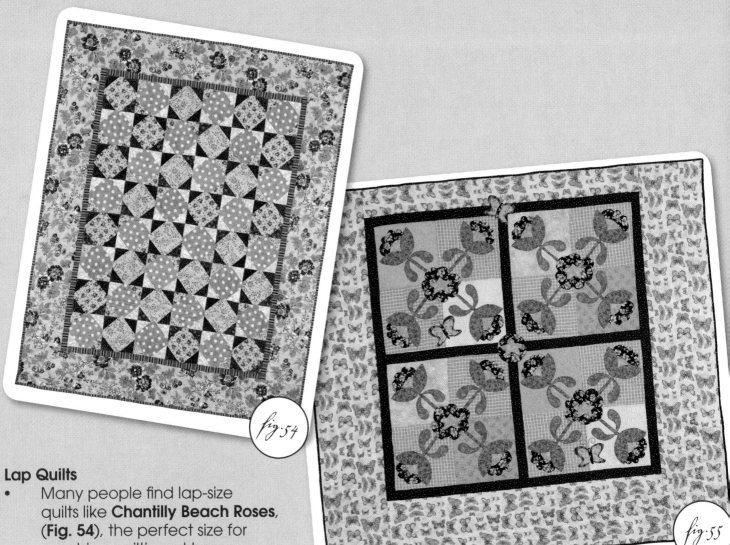

fig·54

fig·55

Lap Quilts

- Many people find lap-size quilts like **Chantilly Beach Roses**, (**Fig. 54**), the perfect size for machine quilting at home.
- When you work on a lap quilt you will need to fan-fold the sides (see **Fig. 56**) to be able to reach the center.
- You may start to experience drag and will learn how to maneuver a larger project.

Tip: I find that lots of quilters never attempt anything larger than lap-size and will have a professional with a long arm machine quilt their bed-size tops — that's always an option.

Bed Quilts

Yes...you really can put a queen size quilt like **Butterfly Garden Quilt**, (**Fig. 55**), *in the opening of your sewing machine. I know — I've done it! My largest quilt was 90" x 90". Here are a few great tips and tricks for working with quilts over 50" wide.*

- I feel quilting a large quilt is a mind game to some extent. You are not putting 90" of quilt in the opening...you only need to get about HALF (50%) of it in there. See, doesn't that sound better?

- To get all that fabric into the center, I fan fold the long sides of the quilt sandwich (**Fig. 56**). I find the fan fold gives me the most flexibility and is the quickest to set up and undo while I'm quilting.

fig. 56

fig. 57

- You will need to fluff the quilt more often to prevent drag with large quilts.
- Another option I highly recommend for quilting full/queen/king size-quilts is to quilt in sections. I used this technique when quilting my **Butterfly Garden Quilt**.

Now that you know all the basics and have had a chance to work on some practice pieces, it's time to pick your project and have some fun free-motion quilting!

Tip: When working on large quilts, I usually quilt the center area first because it is the least amount of fun! Once the center is done, the rest of the quilting goes quickly.

- After folding, slide the quilt package under the presser foot (**Fig. 57**). You may want to loosely fold the end of the quilt that is resting in your lap.

SEW *Simple*

Don't you just love fabric collection swatch packets? The packets feature one square of each fabric in the collection and depending on the manufacturer, they can range from 4 to 10 inches square. Fabric swatches make great table runners! From one packet you can make several table runner centers. Simply add coordinating fabric borders, assemble the table runner envelope-style and you are ready to quilt away!

SEW *Simple*

Finished Block Size: 6" x 6" (15 cm x 15 cm)*
Finished Table Runner Size: 29" x 17" (74 cm x 43 cm)
Featured Quilting Techniques: Loops and Stars and Squiggles

*See **Sew Simple Variations**, page 37, to use a different size swatch or to cut squares from yardage.

FABRIC REQUIREMENTS
Yardage is based on 43"/44" (109/112 cm) wide fabric.

One 6^1/$_2$" x 6^1/$_2$" (17 cm x 17 cm) square **each** of 8 assorted prints
^{3}/$_8$ yd (34 cm) of navy print
^{5}/$_8$ yd (57 cm) of backing fabric

You will also need:
29^1/$_2$" x 17^1/$_2$" (75 cm x 44 cm) rectangle of batting

CUTTING OUT THE PIECES
Follow **Rotary Cutting**, page 73, and **Cutting Diagram (Fig. 1)** to cut fabric. All measurements include ^{1}/$_4$" seam allowances.

From navy print fabric:
- Cut 2 **long borders** 3" x 24^1/$_2$".
- Cut 2 **short borders** 3" x 17^1/$_2$".

From backing fabric:
- Cut 1 **backing rectangle** 17^1/$_2$" x 29^1/$_2$".

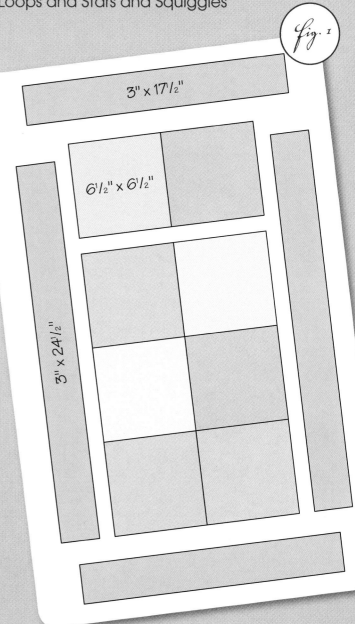

fig. 1

3" x 17^1/$_2$"

6^1/$_2$" x 6^1/$_2$"

3" x 24^1/$_2$"

MAKING THE TABLE RUNNER CENTER

*Refer to **Piecing And Pressing**, page 74, and **Photo**, page 36, to make the table runner.*

1. Sew 4 **squares** together to make a **row**. Make 2 rows.
2. Sew rows together to make **table runner center**.
3. Sew **long borders** to long edges of table runner center. Sew **short borders** to short edges of table runner center to complete **table runner top**.

COMPLETING THE TABLE RUNNER

1. Matching right sides, layer **backing rectangle** (right side up), **table runner top** (right side down), and **batting**. Using a 1/4" seam allowance and leaving an opening for turning, sew layers together. Clip corners; turn right side out and press. Stitch opening closed. Topstitch 1/4" from outer edge around table runner.
2. Follow **Quilting**, page 11, to quilt table runner using the **Quilting Diagram (Fig.2)** as a suggestion. The center blocks of our table runner are quilted with Loops and Stars and there are Squiggles in the borders.

fig. 2

SEW SIMPLE VARIATIONS

This versatile pattern can be made using any size fabric swatches or squares cut from scraps, fat quarters, or yardage. **Note:** *Using larger or smaller squares will make your finished table runner a different size from ours. You may need to purchase additional yardage for borders, backing, and batting if you choose to use larger squares.*

- Cut 8 squares from fabric the desired size or use fabric swatches.
- Follow Steps 1 and 2 of **Making the Table Runner Center**, page 35, to sew squares together.
- Determine your desired finished width for borders and add 1/2" for seam allowances. Measure length through center of table runner and add 1/2" for seam allowances.
- Cut 2 long borders your determined cutting width by determined cutting length. Sew long borders to table runner center.
- Measure width through center of table runner, including added borders, and add 1/2" for seam allowances. Cut 2 short borders your determined cutting width by determined cutting length. Sew short borders to table runner center.
- Follow **Completing The Table Runner**, page 35, to finish and quilt your table runner.

Try This!
To make a unique backing, instead of cutting a rectangle from yardage, simply sew swatches together and trim, if needed, to same size as the table runner top.

THE JOY *of Sewing*

I've sewn since I was in 5th grade and am always attracted to fabric with images of little girls sewing. If you like fabric with sewing themes, too, this fun wall hanging would be the perfect addition to your sewing room or studio! I designed this easy pattern to work with any theme fabric, be it sewing, horses, sports, holidays, etc. The large center square and multiple borders provide lots of open areas to try different quilting techniques.

THE JOY *of Sewing*

Finished Wall Hanging Size: 41" x 43" (104 cm x 109 cm)
Featured Quilting Techniques: Bouncing Hearts, Bubbles, Squiggles, Loops, Outline, and Scallops

FABRIC REQUIREMENTS

Yardage is based on 43"/44" (109/112 cm) wide fabric.

$1/2$ yd (46 cm) of theme print
$1/4$ yd (23 cm) of tan print
$1/2$ yd (46 cm) of red print No. 1
$1/2$ yd (46 cm) of red print No. 2
$5/8$ yd (57 cm) of red print No. 3
$1/2$ yd (46 cm) of black stripe
$2^3/4$ yds (2.5 m) of backing fabric

You will also need:

47" x 49" (119 cm x 124 cm) rectangle of batting

CUTTING OUT THE PIECES

*Follow **Rotary Cutting**, page 73, and **Cutting Diagram (Fig. 1)** to cut fabric. All measurements include $1/4$" seam allowances.*

From theme print:
- Cut 1 strip $12^1/2$"w. From this strip, cut 1 **square** $12^1/2$" x $12^1/2$" (**A**) and 11 **rectangles** $4^1/2$" x $5^1/2$" (**B**).

From tan print:
- Cut 1 strip $3^7/8$"w. From this strip, cut 8 **squares** $3^7/8$" x $3^7/8$" (**C**).
- Cut 1 strip $3^1/2$"w. From this strip, cut 4 **squares** $3^1/2$" x $3^1/2$" (**D**).

From red print No. 1:
- Cut 2 strips $5^1/2$"w. From these strips, cut 11 **rectangles** $4^1/2$" x $5^1/2$" (**E**).
- Cut 1 strip $3^7/8$"w. From this strip, cut 8 **squares** $3^7/8$" x $3^7/8$" (**F**).

From red print No. 2:
- Cut 2 strips $6^1/2$"w. From these strips, cut 29 **rectangles** $2^1/2$" x $6^1/2$" (**G**).

From red print No 3:
- Cut 1 strip $6^1/2$"w. From this strip, cut 4 **outer border corner squares** $6^1/2$" x $6^1/2$" (**H**).
- Cut 2 **top/bottom inner borders** $1^1/2$" x $18^1/2$".
- Cut 2 **side inner borders** $1^1/2$" x $20^1/2$".
- Cut 5 **binding strips** $1^1/2$"w.

From black stripe:
- Cut 2 strips $6^1/2$"w. From these strips, cut 29 **rectangles** $2^1/2$" x $6^1/2$" (**I**).

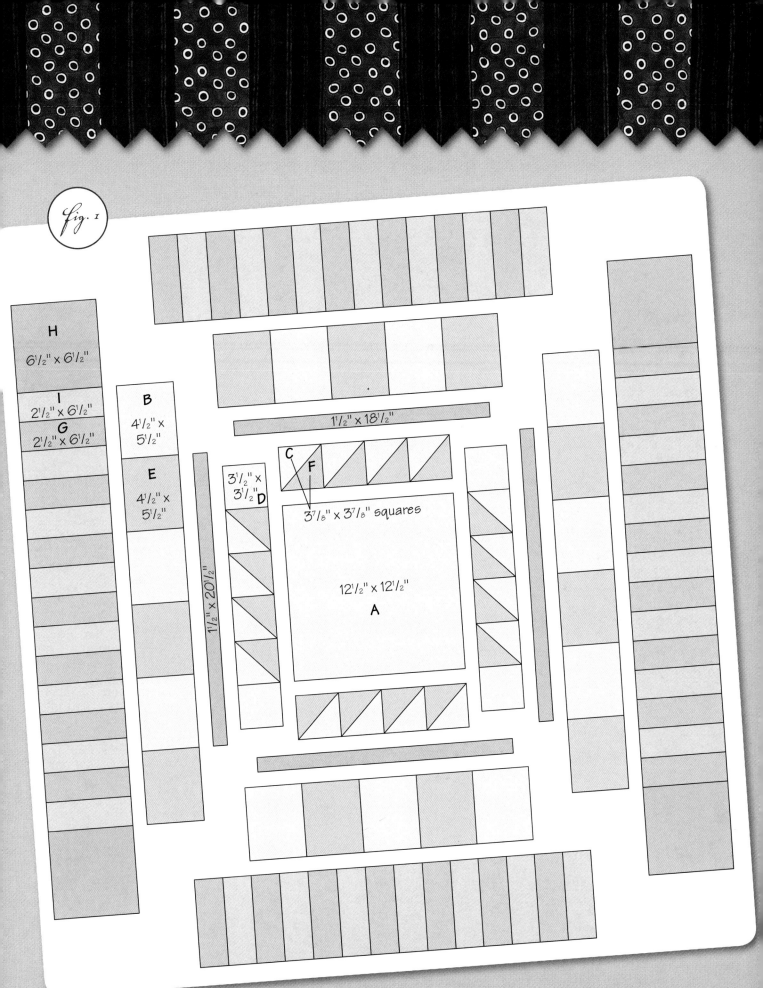

fig. 1

H
6½" × 6½"

I
2½" × 6½"

G
2½" × 6½"

B
4½" × 5½"

E
4½" × 5½"

1½" × 18½"

C
F

3½" × 3½"
D

3⅞" × 3⅞" squares

12½" × 12½"
A

1½" × 20½"

41

ASSEMBLING THE WALL HANGING TOP

*Refer to **Piecing And Pressing**, page 74, and **Photo**, page 45, to make the wall hanging.*

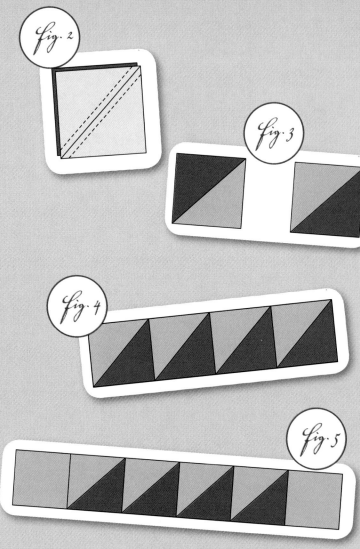

CENTER BLOCK

1. Draw a diagonal line on wrong side of 1 square **C**. With right sides together, place 1 square **C** on top of 1 square **F**. Stitch seam ¼" from each side of drawn line (**Fig. 2**).
2. Cut along drawn line; open and press seam allowances toward darker fabric to make 2 **Triangle-Squares** (**Fig. 3**).
3. Repeat Steps 1 and 2 using remaining **C** and **F** squares to make 16 Triangle-Squares.
4. Sew 4 Triangle-Squares together to make **Unit 1** (**Fig. 4**). Make 4 Unit 1's.
5. Sew 1 Unit 1 to top and bottom edges of square **A**.
6. Sew 1 square **D** to each end of remaining Unit 1's to make 2 **Unit 2's** (**Fig. 5**). Sew 1 Unit 2 to each side of square **A** to make **Center Block** (**Fig. 6**).

INNER BORDER

*Refer to **Photo**, page 45, to add borders to center block.*

1. Sew **top/bottom** and then **side inner borders** to Center Block.

MIDDLE BORDER

1. Alternating placement, match right sides and ***long*** edges to sew 2 rectangles **B** and 3 rectangles **E** together to make **top middle border**.
2. Alternating placement, match right sides and ***long*** edges to sew 3 rectangles **B** and 2 rectangles **E** together to make **bottom middle border**.

3. Alternating placement, match right sides and ***short*** edges to sew 3 rectangles **B** and 3 rectangles **E** together to make **side middle border**. Make 2 side middle borders.
4. Sew top/bottom and then side middle borders to Center Block to make **wall hanging center**.

OUTER BORDER

1. Alternating placement, match right sides and **long** edges to sew 7 rectangles **G** and 7 rectangles **I** together to make **top/bottom border**. Make 2 top/bottom outer borders. Sew top/bottom borders to **wall hanging center**.
2. Alternating placement, match right sides and **long** edges to sew 8 rectangles **G** and 7 rectangles **I** together to make **right side outer border**. Sew 1 square **H** to each end of right side outer border. Sew border to right side of **wall hanging center**.
3. Alternating placement, match right sides and **long** edges to sew 7 rectangles **G** and 8 rectangles **I** together to make **left side outer border**. Sew 1 square **H** to each end of left side outer border. Sew border to left side of **wall hanging center** to make **wall hanging top**.

COMPLETING THE WALL HANGING

1. Following **Quilting**, page 11, to layer and quilt using the **Quilting Diagram (Fig. 7)** as a suggestion. Our wall hanging is quilted with Bouncing Hearts in the center square, Outline quilting in the Triangle-squares, Bubbles in the tan triangles and squares, and Scallops in the red triangles. The inner border is quilted with Scallops and there are Bouncing Hearts in the middle border. The outer border features Squiggles in the red rectangles and Loops in the black rectangles. Bouncing Hearts are quilted in the red corner squares.

2. Follow **Adding a Hanging Sleeve**, page 77, to make and attach a hanging sleeve, if desired.
3. Follow **Binding**, page 77, to bind quilt using binding strips.

fig. 7

45

Sunflowers FOREVER

I have a life-long love of sunflowers! This great little appliquéd sunflower project makes up quickly, providing you with a wall hanging that is the perfect size for practicing your quilting techniques.

Sunflowers FOREVER

Finished Wall Hanging Size: 21" x 29" (53 cm x 74 cm)
Featured Quilting Techniques: Outline, Vines and Leaves, and Sunflowers

FABRIC REQUIREMENTS

Yardage is based on 43"/44" (109/112 cm) wide fabric.

- 1/2 yd (46 cm) of light teal print
- 3/4 yd (69 cm) of teal sunflower print
- 6" x 6" (15 cm x 15 cm) square of red print (pot)
- 5" x 7" (13 cm x 18 cm) rectangle of red plaid (pot rim and medium center)
- 6" x 8" (15 cm x 20 cm) rectangle of green print (leaves)
- 3" x 6" (8 cm x 15 cm) rectangle of brown print (large center)
- 6" x 10" (15 cm x 25 cm) rectangle **each** of 3 gold prints (sunflower petals and small center)
- 7/8 yd (80 cm) of backing fabric

You will also need:

- 27" x 35" (69 cm x 89 cm) rectangle of batting
- 5/8 yd (57 cm) of medium rickrack
- Paper-backed fusible web

CUTTING OUT THE BACKGROUND AND BORDERS

*Follow **Rotary Cutting**, page 73, and **Cutting Diagram (Fig. 1)** to cut fabric. All measurements include 1/4" seam allowances.*

From light teal print:
- Cut 1 **background rectangle** 12 1/2" x 20 1/2".

From teal sunflower print:
- Cut 4 **borders** 4 1/2" x 20 1/2".
- Cut 4 **binding strips** 1 1/2" wide.

From backing fabric:
- Cut 1 **backing rectangle** 27" x 35".

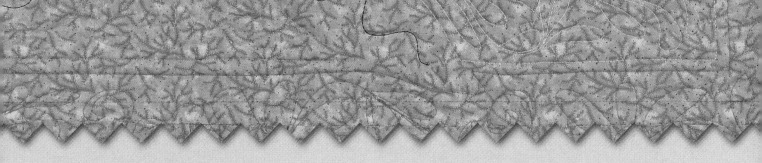

CUTTING OUT THE APPLIQUES

*Refer to **Preparing Fusible Appliqués**, page 75, to use patterns, pages 52 and 53.*

From red print:
- Cut 1 **pot.**

From red plaid:
- Cut 1 **pot rim.**
- Cut 1 **medium center.**

From green print:
- Cut 1 **leaf.** Cut 1 **leaf reversed.**

From brown print:
- Cut 1 **large center.**

From gold prints:
- Cut 11 **petals.**
- Cut 1 **small center.**

ASSEMBLING THE WALL HANGING TOP

*Refer to **Wall Hanging Top Diagram** (**Fig. 2**), page 50, for placement. Follow **Piecing And Pressing**, page 74, and **Machine Blanket Stitch Appliqué**, page 76, for techniques.*

1. Sew 1 **border** to each side of the **background rectangle.**
2. Sew the remaining **borders** to the top and bottom of the background rectangle to make **wall hanging top.**
3. Position **pot** and **pot rim** on wall hanging top.
4. Tucking one raw end under pot rim, position **rickrack** to form stem; pin in place. Fuse pot and pot rim. Straight stitch through center of stem.
5. Position, and then fuse **leaves**, **petals**, **large**, **medium**, and **small centers**.
6. Using matching thread, Blanket Stitch around appliqués.

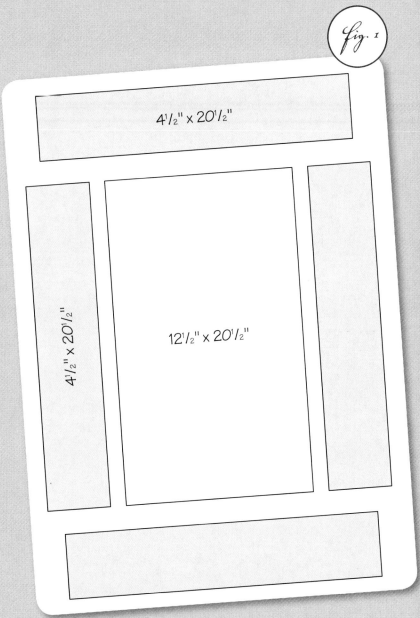

fig. 1

4¹⁄₂" x 20¹⁄₂"

4¹⁄₂" x 20¹⁄₂"

12¹⁄₂" x 20¹⁄₂"

fig. 2

COMPLETING THE WALL HANGING

1. Following **Quilting**, page 11, to layer and quilt using the **Quilting Diagram (Fig. 3)** as a suggestion. Our wall hanging has outline quilting around the appliqués. The background rectangle is quilted with vines and leaves and the border with sunflowers.
2. Follow **Adding a Hanging Sleeve**, page 77, to make and attach a hanging sleeve, if desired.
3. Follow **Binding**, page 77, to bind quilt using binding strips.

fig. 3

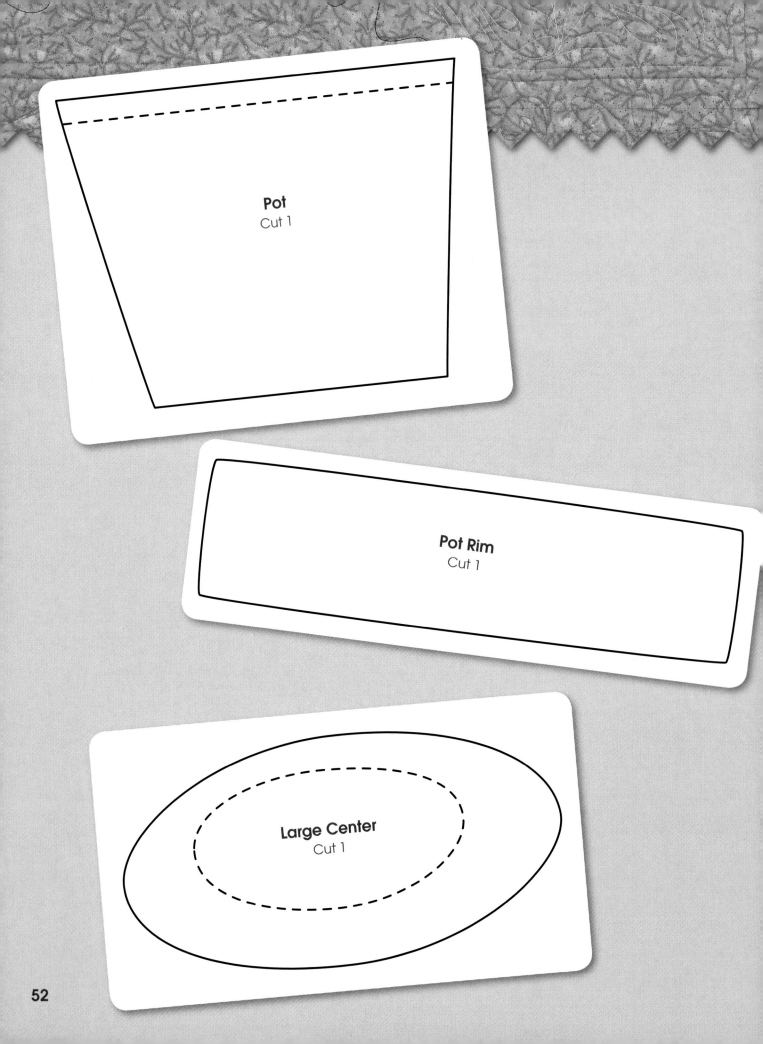

Pot
Cut 1

Pot Rim
Cut 1

Large Center
Cut 1

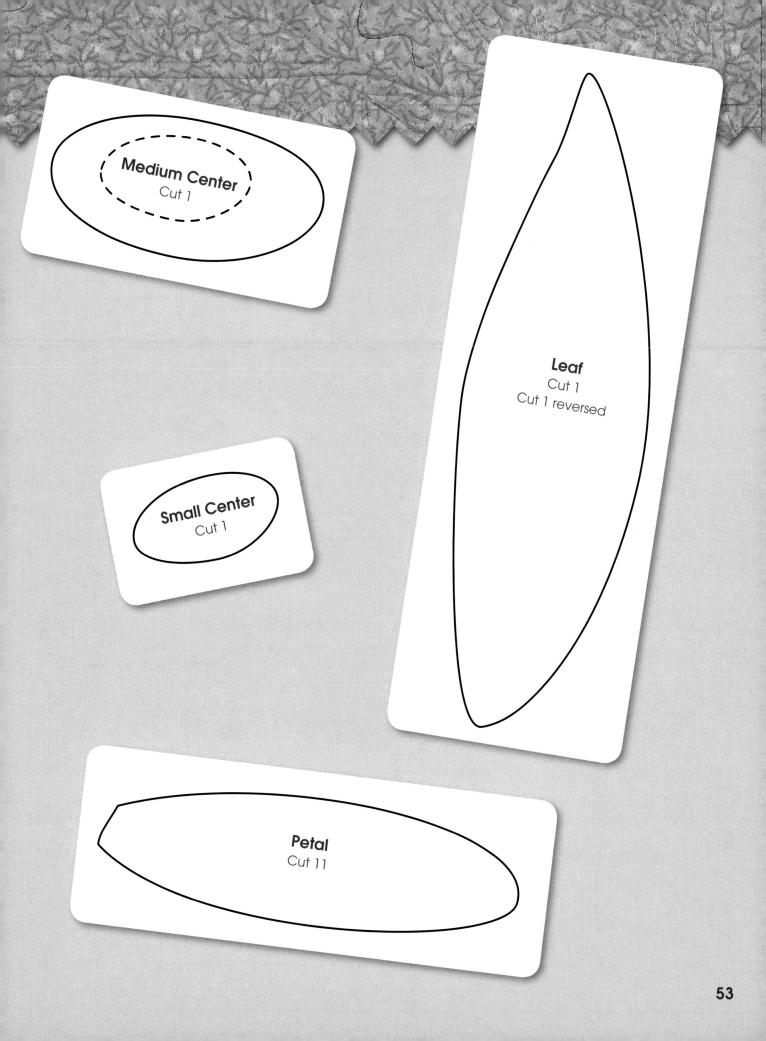

Medium Center
Cut 1

Leaf
Cut 1
Cut 1 reversed

Small Center
Cut 1

Petal
Cut 11

Chantilly Beach ROSES

Some fabrics call your name and you really feel the need to make a quilt with them. The border print and the polka dot fabrics in this quilt did just that to me. Although purchased at different times, I think they work very well together. The coordinating teal and red prints I used for the Snowball Blocks really tie all the fabrics together. This fast and easy throw-size quilt is the perfect project to use and enjoy those "must have" fabrics!

Chantilly Beach ROSES

Finished Throw Size: 53" x 65" (135 cm x 165 cm)
Finished Block Size: 6" x 6" (15 cm x 15 cm)
Featured Quilting Techniques: Roses, Leaves and Swirls, Loops, and Squiggles

FABRIC REQUIREMENTS

Yardage is based on 43"/44" (109/112 cm) wide fabric.

$7/8$ yd (80 cm) of teal/ green polka dot print

$5/8$ yd (57 cm) *each* of teal prints No. 1 and 2

$1/4$ yd (23 cm) *each* of teal prints No. 3 and 4

$3/8$ yd (34 cm) *each* of 3 different red prints

$5/8$ yd (57 cm) of red/green stripe

$1 5/8$ yds (1.5 m) of teal floral print

4 yds (3.7 m) of backing fabric

You will also need:

59" x 71" (150 cm x 180 cm) rectangle of batting

CUTTING OUT THE PIECES

*Follow **Rotary Cutting**, page 73, and **Cutting Diagram (Fig. 1)** to cut fabric. All measurements include $1/4$" seam allowances. Cutting lengths for outer borders include an extra 2" for "insurance," and will be trimmed to fit after measuring quilt top center.*

From teal/green polka dot print:
- Cut 4 strips $6 1/2$"w. From these strips, cut 24 **large squares** $6 1/2$" x $6 1/2$".

From each of teal prints No. 1 and 2:
- Cut 2 strips $6 1/2$"w. From these strips, cut 12 **large squares** $6 1/2$" x $6 1/2$" for a *total* of 24 large squares.

From *each* of teal prints No. 1, 2, 3, and 4:
- Cut 2 strips 3"w. From these strips, cut 24 **small squares** 3" x 3" for a *total* of 96 small squares.

From *each* red print:
- Cut 3 strips 3"w. From these strips, cut 32 **small squares** 3" x 3" for a total of 96 small squares.

From red and green stripe:
- Cut 5 **inner border strips** $1 1/2$"w.
- Cut 7 **binding strips** $1 1/2$"w.

From teal floral print:
- Cut 2 *lengthwise* **side outer borders** $7 1/2$" x $52 1/2$".
- Cut 2 *lengthwise* **top/bottom outer borders** $7 1/2$" x $54 1/2$".

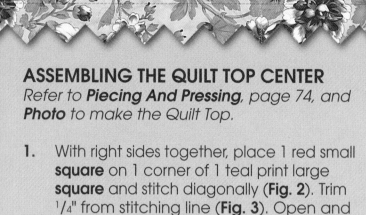

ASSEMBLING THE QUILT TOP CENTER
*Refer to **Piecing And Pressing**, page 74, and **Photo** to make the Quilt Top.*

1. With right sides together, place 1 red small **square** on 1 corner of 1 teal print large **square** and stitch diagonally (**Fig. 2**). Trim 1/4" from stitching line (**Fig. 3**). Open and press seam allowances toward darker fabric (**Fig. 4**).
2. Repeat Step 1 to add a red small **square** to each remaining corner of teal print **large square** to make **Snowball Block A** (**Fig. 5**). Make 24 Snowball Block A's.
3. Repeat Steps 1 and 2 using teal **small squares** and polka dot **large squares** to make **Snowball Block B** (**Fig. 6**). Make 24 Snowball Block B's.
4. Alternating Snowball Blocks A and B, sew 6 **blocks** together to make a **row**. Make 8 rows.
5. Sew rows together to make **quilt top center**.

ADDING THE BORDERS
1. To add **top/bottom inner borders**, measure width across center of quilt top center. From 2 inner border strips, cut 2 inner borders this measurement. Sew 1 inner border to top and bottom edges of quilt top center.
2. To add **side inner borders**, sew remaining inner border strips together end to end to make 1 continuous border strip. Measure length across center of quilt top center, including added top/bottom inner borders. From continuous border strip, cut 2 side inner borders this measurement. Sew 1 side inner border to each side of quilt top center.

3. Measure length across center of quilt top center. Trim **side outer borders**, to this measurement. Sew side outer borders to the quilt top center.
4. Measure width across center of quilt top center, including side outer borders. Trim **top/bottom outer borders**, to this measurement. Sew top/bottom outer borders to the quilt top center.

COMPLETING THE QUILT
1. Following **Quilting**, page 11, to layer and quilt using the **Quilting Diagram (Fig. 7)** as a suggestion. Our throw is quilted with a Rose in the center and Leaves in the corners of each Snowball Block. The inner border is quilted with a Squiggle and the outer border features Roses, Leaves, and Swirls.
2. Follow **Adding a Hanging Sleeve**, page 77, to make and attach a hanging sleeve, if desired.
3. Follow **Binding**, page 77, to bind quilt using binding strips.

fig. 7

Butterfly Garden QUILT & PILLOW SHAMS

In my garden I have two very large butterfly bushes, which I adore. They are usually covered with yellow, black, and orange butterflies. Everyone is amazed when they see how many butterflies visit me! I wanted to capture that feeling in a bed size quilt and matching quilted pillow shams.

Butterfly Garden QUILT

Finished Quilt Size: 87" x 79" (221 cm x 201 cm)
Finished Block Size: 26" x 26" (66 cm x 66 cm)
Featured Quilting Techniques: Outline, Swirls, and Continuous Curls

FABRIC REQUIREMENTS

Yardage is based on 43"/44" (109/112 cm) wide fabric.

- 4^1/$_4$ yds (3.9 m) of butterfly print
- 1^3/$_4$ yds (1.6 m) of tan plaid
- ^{1}/$_2$ yd (46 cm) *each* of 4 tan prints
- 1^7/$_8$ yds (1.7 m) of red print
- 1 yd (91 m) of black print (flowers, circle, and butterfly bodies)
- ^{1}/$_2$ yd (46 cm) of gold print (flower centers and stars)
- 1^1/$_8$ yds (1 m) of green print No. 1 (stems and large leaves)
- ^{3}/$_4$ yd (69 cm) of green print No. 2 (small leaves)
- 12" x 15" (30 cm x 38 cm) rectangle of pink stripe (large butterfly wings)
- 10" x 13" (25 cm x 33 cm) rectangle of pink print (small butterfly wings)
- 7^1/$_4$ yds (6.7 m) of backing fabric

You will also need:

- 104" x 84" (264 cm x 213 cm) rectangle of batting
- Paper-backed fusible web

CUTTING OUT THE BACKGROUND AND BORDERS

*Follow **Rotary Cutting**, page 73, and **Cutting Diagram (Fig. 1)** to cut fabric. All measurements include ^{1}/$_4$" seam allowances.*

From butterfly print:
- Cut 2 **side borders** 14^1/$_2$" x 78^1/$_2$".
- Cut 1 **bottom border** 14^1/$_2$" x 58^1/$_2$".
- Cut 1 **top border** 6^1/$_2$" x 58^1/$_2$".

From tan plaid:
- Cut 4 strips 13^1/$_2$" w. From these strips, cut 8 **background squares** 13^1/$_2$" x 13^1/$_2$".

From *each* tan print:
- Cut 2 **background squares** 13^1/$_2$" x 13^1/$_2$".

From red print:
- Cut 2 **long sashing strips** 2^1/$_2$" x 58^1/$_2$".
- Cut 3 **medium sashing strips** 2^1/$_2$" x 54^1/$_2$".
- Cut 2 **short sashing strips** 2^1/$_2$" x 26^1/$_2$".
- Cut 8 **binding strips** 2^1/$_2$" x 26^1/$_2$".

From backing fabric and batting:
- Cut 1 **rectangle** 64" x 84".
- Cut 2 **rectangles** 20" x 84".

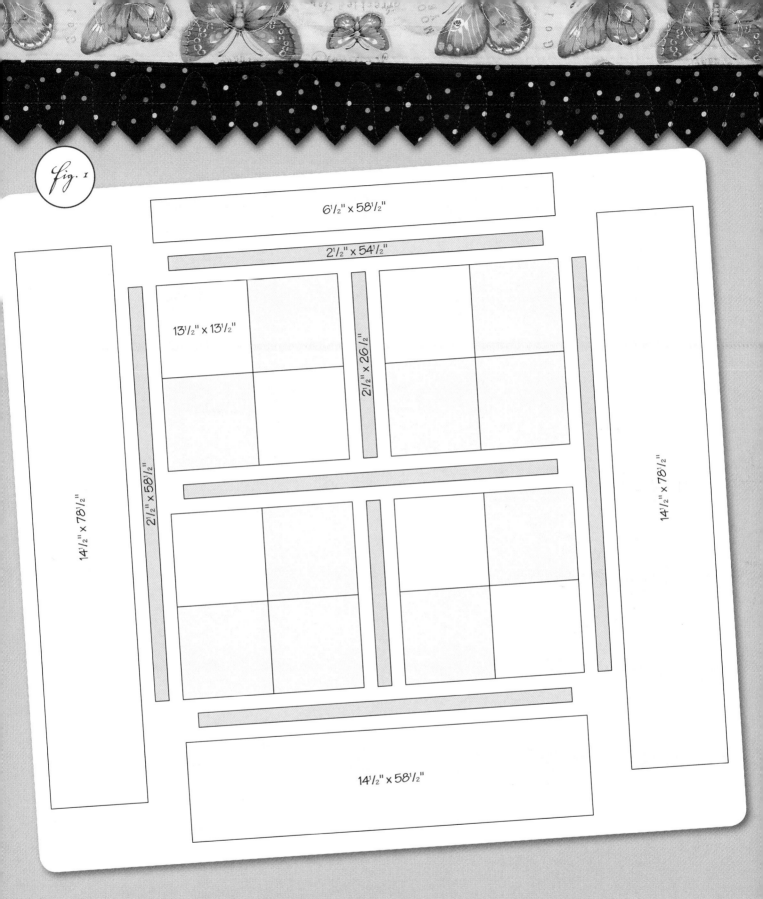

Fig. 1

6½" x 58½"

2½" x 54½"

13½" x 13½"

2½" x 26½"

2½" x 58½"

14½" x 78½"

14½" x 78½"

14½" x 58½"

CUTTING OUT THE APPLIQUES

Refer to ***Preparing Fusible Appliqués****,
page 75, to use patterns, pages 67-70.*

From black print:
- Cut 4 large flowers (**C**).
- Cut 16 small flowers (**D**).
- Cut 3 butterfly bodies (**K**).
- Cut 1 circle (**H**).

From gold print:
- Cut 16 flower centers (**E**).
- Cut 5 stars (**G**).

From green print No. 1:
- Cut 16 stems 7" x ¹/₂" (**B**).
- Cut 32 large leaves (**F**).

From green print No. 2:
- Cut 16 small leaves (**A**). Cut 16 small leaves reversed (**Ar**).

From pink stripe:
- Cut 3 outer butterfly wings (**I**).

From pink print:
- Cut 3 inner butterfly wings (**J**).

ASSEMBLING THE BLOCKS

Refer to ***Photo****, page 66, for placement.
Follow* ***Piecing And Pressing****, page 74, and*
Machine Blanket Stitch Appliqué*, page 76,
for technique.*

1. Sew 2 tan plaid and 2 tan print **background squares** together to make **block background**. Make 4 block backgrounds.
2. Fold each block background in half diagonally both directions and finger press folds; unfold. Using seam and fold lines as placement guides, position appliqué pieces **A-G** on block backgrounds; fuse (**Fig. 2**).
3. Using matching thread, Blanket Stitch around appliqués.

ASSEMBLING THE QUILT TOP CENTER

1. Orienting the blocks to keep the tan plaid squares in the left top and bottom right corners, sew 2 **blocks** and 1 **short sashing strip** together to make a **row** (**Fig. 3**). Make 2 rows.
2. Sew the 3 **medium sashing strips** and 2 rows together to make **Unit 1**.
3. Sew 1 **long sashing strip** to each side of Unit 1 to make **Unit 2**.
4. Sew the **top** and **bottom borders** to Unit 2 to make **quilt top center**. **Note:** Side borders are not attached at this time.
5. Position appliqué pieces **H** and **G** in center of quilt top center; fuse. Position appliqué pieces **I-K** on block backgrounds and top border; fuse.
6. Using matching thread, Blanket Stitch around appliqués.

fig. 2

fig. 3

COMPLETING THE QUILT

1. Following **Quilting**, page 11, to layer and quilt the **quilt top center** and **side borders** using the **Quilting Diagram** (**Fig. 4**) as a suggestion. **Note:** Do not quilt into the 1/4" seam allowances of the **quilt top center** and **side borders**. Our quilt top center has Outline quilting around the appliqués, Swirls in the backgrounds, and a Continuous Swirl in the sashings. The borders are quilted with larger Swirls. The butterfly antenna are formed by repeating the V-curl shape several times with straight stitches (**Fig. 5**).

2. Trim the backing and batting of the quilt top center and side borders even with the quilt tops.

3. Cut 2 "seam covers" 1 1/2" x 78 1/2" from backing fabric. Press 1 long edge of each seam cover 1/4" to the wrong side.

4. Mark the center of each side of the quilt top center, one side of each side border, and the raw edge of each seam cover.

5. Referring to **Fig. 6** and matching center marks, corners, and raw edges and easing in any fullness, layer and pin **quilt top center** (right side up), 1 **side border** (right side down) and 1 **seam cover** (right side down).

6. Using a walking foot, sew layers together through all thicknesses. To reduce bulk, trim batting from seam allowances close to stitching. Press seam allowances open.

7. Press seam cover over seam allowances and blindstitch to quilt back along folded edge (**Fig. 7**).

8. Repeat Steps 5 -7 to sew remaining border to quilt top center.

9. Follow **Binding**, page 77, to bind quilt using binding strips.

fig. 4

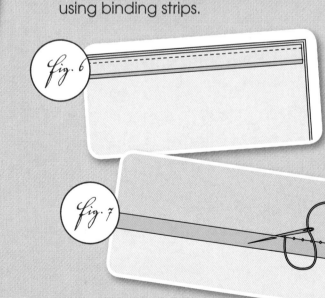

fig. 6

fig. 7

fig. 5

Tip: I find if I use backing fabric with lots of pattern you don't notice that seam covers are used. I've also done the seam covers in contrasting fabric for a design element.

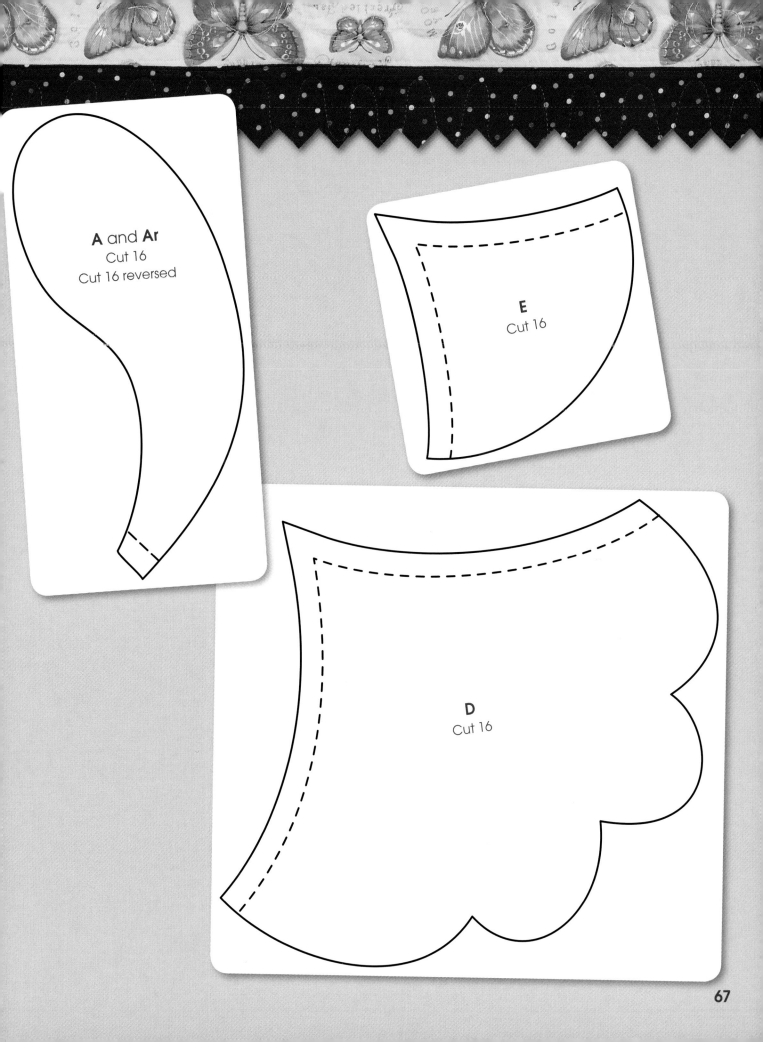

A and **Ar**
Cut 16
Cut 16 reversed

E
Cut 16

D
Cut 16

C
Cut 4

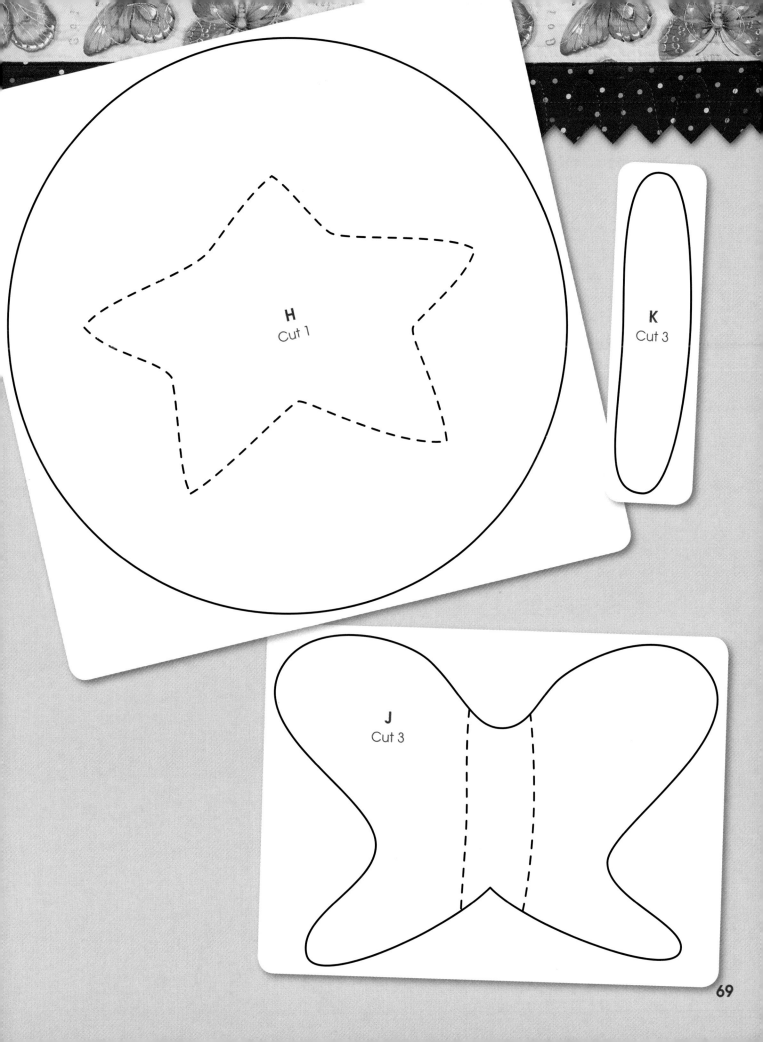

H
Cut 1

K
Cut 3

J
Cut 3

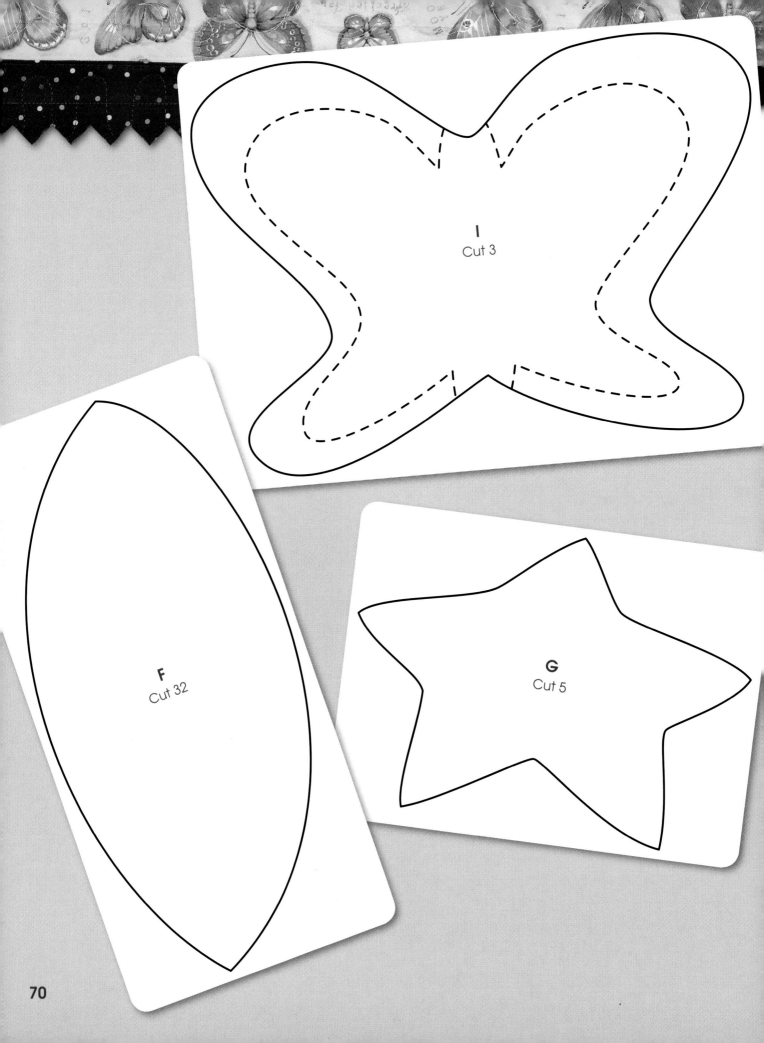

I
Cut 3

F
Cut 32

G
Cut 5

70

Butterfly Garden
PILLOW SHAMS

Finished Pillow Sham Size: 30¹/₂" x 25¹/₂" (77 cm x 65 cm)
Featured Quilting Techniques: Swirls, In-The-Ditch, and Squiggles

FABRIC REQUIREMENTS

Yardage is based on 43"/44" (109/112 cm) wide fabric and includes enough for **two** *pillow shams.*

    2⁵/₈ yds (2.4 m) of butterfly print
    1¹/₂ yds (1.4 m) of red print
You will also need:
    27" x 63" (69 cm x 160 cm) rectangle
    of batting

CUTTING OUT THE PIECES

Follow **Rotary Cutting,** *page 73, and* **Cutting and Assembly Diagram (Fig. 1)** *to cut fabric. All measurements include* ¹/₄" *seam allowances.*

From butterfly print:
- Cut 2 **front rectangles** 26" x 21".
- Cut 4 **back rectangles** 15¹/₂" x 21".

From red print:
- Cut 16 **border strips** 3" x 26".

From batting:
- Cut 2 **rectangles** 30¹/₂" x 25¹/₂".

fig. 1

3" x 26"

3" x 26"

26" x 21"

ASSEMBLING THE PILLOW SHAMS

*Refer to **Piecing And Pressing**, page 74, to make the pillow shams.*

SHAM FRONTS
1. Sew 1 **border strip** to each long edge of each **front rectangle**.
2. Sew 1 **border strip** to remaining edges of each front rectangle to make 2 **sham fronts**.
3. Layer 1 **sham front** and 1 **batting rectangle**. Repeat with remaining sham front and batting rectangle.
4. Follow **Quilting**, page 11 and **Quilting Diagram (Fig. 2)** to quilt center section, *only*, of sham fronts. Our pillow sham center sections are quilted with Swirls.

SHAM BACKS
1. On each **back rectangle**, press 1 long edge ¹/₄" to the wrong side; press ¹/₄" to the wrong side again and stitch in place.
2. With right sides facing up, overlap hemmed edges of 2 back rectangles to make a 26" x 21" **rectangle**. Baste together at overlap. Repeat with remaining back rectangles.
3. Sew 1 **border strip** to each long edge of each rectangle.
4. Sew 1 **border strip** to remaining edges of each rectangle to make 2 **sham backs**.

COMPLETING THE PILLOW SHAMS
1. Matching right sides, layer 1 **sham front** and 1 **sham back**. Using a ¹/₄" seam allowance and leaving an opening for turning, sew layers together. Clip corners; remove basting threads. Turn right side out and press. Stitch opening closed. Topstitch ¹/₄" from outer edge around **pillow sham**. Repeat using remaining sham front and back.
2. Our pillow shams are stitched In-The-Ditch between the center sections and borders. There are Squiggles quilted in the borders.

fig. 2

GENERAL *Instructions*

FABRICS
SELECTING FABRICS
Choose high-quality, medium-weight 100% cotton fabrics. All-cotton fabrics hold a crease better, fray less, and are easier to quilt than cotton/polyester blends.

Yardage requirements listed for each project are based on 43"/44" wide fabric with a "usable" width of 40" after shrinkage and trimming selvages. Actual usable width will probably vary slightly from fabric to fabric. Our recommended yardage lengths should be adequate for occasional re-squaring of fabric when many cuts are required.

PREPARING FABRICS
We recommend that all fabrics be washed, dried, and pressed before cutting. If fabrics are not pre-washed, washing the finished quilt will cause shrinkage and give it a more "antiqued" look and feel. Bright and dark colors, which may run, should always be washed before cutting. After washing and drying fabric, fold lengthwise with wrong sides together and matching selvages.

ROTARY CUTTING
Rotary cutting has brought speed and accuracy to quiltmaking by allowing quilters to easily cut strips of fabric and then cut those strips into smaller pieces.

- Place fabric on work surface with fold closest to you.

- Square left edge of fabric using rotary cutter and rulers (**Figs. 1** and **2**).

- Cut all strips from the selvage-to-selvage width of the fabric unless otherwise indicated in project instructions.

- To cut each strip required for a project, place ruler over cut edge of fabric, aligning desired marking on ruler with cut edge; make cut (**Fig. 3**).

- When cutting several strips from a single piece of fabric, it is important to make sure that cuts remain at a perfect right angle to the fold; square fabric as needed.

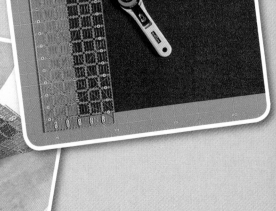

fig. 1

fig. 2

fig. 3

PIECING AND PRESSING

Precise cutting, followed by accurate piecing and pressing will ensure that all pieces of quilt top fit together well.

PIECING

- Set sewing machine stitch length for approximately 11 stitches per inch.

- Use neutral-colored general-purpose sewing thread (not quilting thread) in needle and in bobbin.

- An accurate 1/4" seam allowance is *essential*. Presser feet that are 1/4" wide are available for most sewing machines.

- When piecing, always place pieces right sides together and match raw edges; pin if necessary.

- Chain piecing saves time and will usually result in more accurate piecing.

- Trim away points of seam allowances that extend beyond edges of sewn pieces.

Sewing Across Seam Intersections

When sewing across intersection of two seams, place pieces right sides together and match seams exactly, making sure seam allowances are pressed in opposite directions (**Fig. 4**).

Sewing Sharp Points

To ensure sharp points when joining triangular or diagonal pieces, stitch across the center of the "X" (shown in pink) formed on wrong side by previous seams (**Fig. 5**).

PRESSING

- Use steam iron set on "Cotton" for all pressing.

- Press after sewing each seam.

- Seam allowances are almost always pressed to one side, usually toward darker fabric. However, to reduce bulk it may occasionally be necessary to press seam allowances toward the lighter fabric or even to press them open.

- To prevent dark fabric seam allowance from showing through light fabric, trim darker seam allowance slightly narrower than lighter seam allowance.

- To press long seams, such as those in long strip sets, without curving or other distortion, lay strips across width of the ironing board.

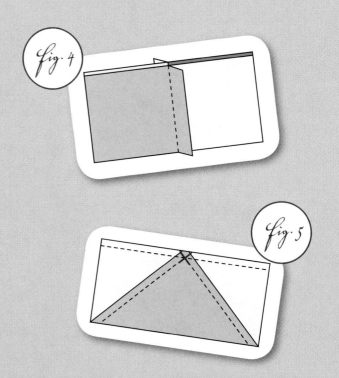

fig. 4

fig. 5

APPLIQUÉ
PREPARING FUSIBLE APPLIQUÉS

Patterns for fused appliqués are printed in reverse to enable you to use our speedy method of preparing appliqués by following Steps 1 – 4 (below). Dashed lines on patterns indicate overlap. If the instructions call for a pattern to be cut in reverse, it is because the shape will be used facing both directions. Use a black fine-point marker to trace the pattern onto plain white paper, flip paper over and then follow Steps 1 – 4 to trace pattern onto web from the "wrong" side of the paper.

fig. 6

fig. 7

fig. 8

1. Place paper-backed fusible web, web side down, over appliqué pattern. Use a pencil to trace pattern onto paper side of web as many times as indicated in project instructions for a single fabric. Repeat for additional patterns and fabrics. (**Note:** Some pieces may be given as measurements, such as a 2" x 4" rectangle, instead of drawn patterns. Draw shape onto paper side of web using a ruler.)

2. To reduce stiffness when appliquéing, cut away the center of the fusible web 1/4" inside the traced line. Do not cut on the line (**Fig. 6**). It may not be necessary to cut away the center of small or narrow pieces.

3. Follow manufacturer's instructions to fuse traced patterns to wrong side of fabrics. Do not remove paper backing.

4. Cut out appliqué pieces along traced lines (**Fig. 7**). Remove paper backing from all pieces (**Fig. 8**).

MACHINE BLANKET STITCH APPLIQUÉ

Some sewing machines feature a Blanket Stitch similar to the one used in this book. Refer to your owner's manual for machine set-up. If your machine does not have this stitch, try any of the decorative stitches your machine has until you are satisfied with the look.

1. Thread sewing machine and bobbin with 100% cotton thread in desired weight.
2. Attach an open-toe presser foot. Select far right needle position and needle down (if your machine has these features).
3. If desired, pin a commercial stabilizer to wrong side of background fabric or spray wrong side of background fabric with starch to stabilize.
4. Bring bobbin thread to the top of the fabric by lowering then raising the needle, bringing up the bobbin thread loop. Pull the loop all the way to the surface.
5. Begin by stitching 5 or 6 stitches in place (drop feed dogs or set stitch length at 0), or use your machine's lock stitch feature, if equipped, to anchor thread. Return setting to selected Blanket Stitch.
6. Most of the Blanket Stitch should be done on the appliqué with the right edges of the stitch falling at the very outside edge of the appliqué. Stitch over all exposed raw edges of appliqué pieces.
7. (**Note:** Dots on **Figs. 9 – 14** indicate where to leave needle in fabric when pivoting.) Always stopping with needle down in background fabric, refer to **Fig. 9** to stitch outside points like tips of leaves. Stop one stitch short of point. Raise presser foot. Pivot project slightly, lower presser foot, and make one angled **Stitch 1**. Take next stitch, stop at point, and pivot so **Stitch 2** will be perpendicular to point. Pivot slightly to make **Stitch 3**. Continue stitching.
8. For outside corners (**Fig. 10**), stitch to corner, stopping with needle in background fabric. Raise presser foot. Pivot project, lower presser foot, and take an angled stitch. Raise presser foot. Pivot project, lower presser foot and stitch adjacent side.
9. For inside corners (**Fig. 11**), stitch to the corner, taking the last bite at corner and stopping with the needle down in background fabric. Raise presser foot. Pivot project, lower presser foot, and take an angled stitch. Raise presser foot. Pivot project, lower presser foot and stitch adjacent side.

fig. 9

fig. 10

fig. 11

10. When stitching outside curves (**Fig. 12**), stop with needle down in background fabric. Raise presser foot and pivot project as needed. Lower presser foot and continue stitching, pivoting as often as necessary to follow curve. Small circles may require pivoting between each stitch.

11. When stitching inside curves (**Fig. 13**), stop with needle down in background fabric. Raise presser foot and pivot project as needed. Lower presser foot and continue stitching, pivoting as often as necessary to follow curve.

12. When stopping stitching, use a lock stitch to sew 5 or 6 stitches in place or use a needle to pull threads to wrong side of background fabric (**Fig. 14**); knot, then trim ends.

13. Carefully tear away stabilizer, if used.

ADDING A HANGING SLEEVE

Attaching a hanging sleeve to back of wall hanging or quilt before the binding is added allows your project to be displayed on a wall.

1. Measure width of quilt top edge and subtract 1". Cut piece of fabric 7"w by determined measurement.

2. Press short edges of fabric piece ¹/₄" to wrong side; press edges ¹/₄" to wrong side again and machine stitch in place.

3. Matching wrong sides, fold piece in half lengthwise to form tube.

4. Before sewing binding to quilt, match raw edges and pin hanging sleeve to center top edge on back of quilt.

5. Bind quilt, treating hanging sleeve as part of backing.

6. Blindstitch bottom of hanging sleeve to backing, taking care not to stitch through to front of quilt.

Tip: Instead of pins, I use water-soluble glue to hold the sleeve to the quilt so I don't have to work around pins when attaching the binding.

BINDING
MAKING STRAIGHT-GRAIN BINDING

1. With right sides together and using diagonal seams (**Fig. 15**), sew the short ends of the binding strips together, if needed, to achieve the necessary length.

2. Press seam allowances open. Press one long edge of binding ¹/₄" to the wrong side.

PAT'S MACHINE-SEWN BINDING

For a quick and easy finish when attaching straight-grain binding with overlapped corners, Pat sews her binding to the back of the quilt and Machine Blanket Stitches it in place on the front, eliminating all hand stitching.

1. Using a narrow zigzag, stitch around quilt top close to the raw edges (**Fig. 16**). Trim backing and batting even with edges of quilt top.
2. Matching unfolded edge of binding with raw edges of quilt top and using a ¹/₄" seam allowance, sew a length of binding to top and bottom edges on **wrong** side of quilt.
3. Fold binding over to quilt front and pin pressed edges in place, covering stitching line (**Fig. 17**); Blanket Stitch binding close to pressed edge. Trim ends of top and bottom binding even with edges of quilt top.
4. Leaving approximately 1¹/₂" of binding at each end, stitch a length of binding to wrong side of each side of quilt (**Fig. 18**).
5. Trim each end of binding ¹/₂" longer than bound edge. Fold under each raw end of binding (**Fig. 19**); pin in place. Fold binding over to quilt front and Blanket Stitch in place, as in **Step 3**.

SIGNING AND DATING YOUR QUILT

A completed quilt is a work of art and should be signed and dated. A label should reflect the style of the quilt, the occasion or person for which it was made, and the quilter's own particular talents. Hand stitch your completed label to the back of your quilt. Some suggestions are:

* Embroider quilter's name, date, and any additional information on quilt top or backing. Matching floss will leave a subtle record. Bright or contrasting floss will make the information stand out.
* Make label from muslin and use permanent marker to write information. Use different colored permanent markers to make label more decorative.
* Use photo-transfer paper to add an image to a white or cream fabric label.
* Piece an extra block from quilt top pattern to use as label. Add information with permanent fabric pen.

fig. 16

fig. 17

fig. 18

fig. 19

- Write a message on an appliquéd design from quilt top.
- Use your leftover binding strips or fabric to frame your label.

Tip: I use basting glue to temporarily hold labels in place. This really keeps the label straight while I'm stitching and I don't have to work around pins.

TIPS FOR MAKING AWARD WINNING QUILTS

The basics I have given you are stepping-stones to making competition quilts that win awards. If you want to take your machine quilting to the highest level of excellence for competition here are a few more tips.

- Lock stitches need to be invisible and lump free as possible. Practice starting and stopping in the ditch.
- Instead of starting and stopping with a lock stitch, just start stitching, take the thread ends to the back, hand tie them and hide the ends in the batting.
- Stitching must be of an even density across the quilt.
- Stitch length needs to be very even.

Credits:

Thanks to P&B Textiles for many of the beautiful fabrics featured in these projects, Janome for providing my sewing machine, and Mountain Mist for suppling an assortment of batting. To make the projects I used Mettler® thread, Mountain Mist® batting, and HeatnBond Lite® fusible web.

Production Team:

Technical Editor
Lisa Lancaster
Technical/Editorial Writer
Jean Lewis
Graphic Designer
Dayle Carozza
Production Artists
Amy Gerke and
Frances Huddleston
Photography Stylist
Christy Myers

ISBN-13: 978-1-60140-510-4
ISBN-10: 1-60140-510-3

Metric Conversion Chart

Inches x 2.54 = centimeters (cm)
Inches x 25.4 = millimeters (mm)
Inches x .0254 = meters (m)

Yards x .9144 = meters (m)
Yards x 91.44 = centimeters (cm)
Centimeters x .3937 = inches (")
Meters x 1.0936 = yards (yd)

Standard Equivalents

1/8"	3.2 mm	0.32 cm	1/8 yard	11.43 cm	0.11 m
1/4"	6.35 mm	0.635 cm	1/4 yard	22.86 cm	0.23 m
3/8"	9.5 mm	0.95 cm	3/8 yard	34.29 cm	0.34 m
1/2"	12.7 mm	1.27 cm	1/2 yard	45.72 cm	0.46 m
5/8"	15.9 mm	1.59 cm	5/8 yard	57.15 cm	0.57 m
3/4"	19.1 mm	1.91 cm	3/4 yard	68.58 cm	0.69 m
7/8"	22.2 mm	2.22 cm	7/8 yard	80 cm	0.8 m
1"	25.4 mm	2.54 cm	1 yard	91.44 cm	0.91 m

LOOK FOR THESE OTHER LEISURE ARTS PUBLICATIONS

by Pat Sloan

Leaflet #3649

Leaflet #4389

Leaflet #3784

Leaflet #4122

Leaflet #3874